DECODING YOUR DREAMS

DECODING YOUR DREAMS

Ray Douglas

Illustrations by
Steinar Lund & Lynne Milton

STERLING PUBLISHING CO., INC.
NEW YORK

Library of Congress Cataloging-in-Publication Data

Douglas, Ray.
    Decoding your dreams / Ray Douglas ; illustrated by Steinar Lund &
Lynne Milton.
        p. cm.
    Includes index.
    ISBN 1-4027-2282-6
    1. Dream interpretation. I. Title.

BF1091.D665 2005
154.6'3--dc22

2005023762

2   4   6   8   10   9   7   5   3   1

Published by Sterling Publishing Co., Inc.
387 Park Avenue South, New York, NY 10016
© 2005 by Ray Douglas
Distributed in Canada by Sterling Publishing
^c/o Canadian Manda Group, 165 Dufferin Street
Toronto, Ontario, Canada M6K 3H6
Distributed in the United Kingdom by GMC Distribution Services,
Castle Place, 166 High Street, Lewes, East Sussex, England BN7 1XU
Distributed in Australia by Capricorn Link (Australia) Pty. Ltd.
P.O. Box 704, Windsor, NSW 2756, Australia

Printed in China
Sterling ISBN 13: 978-1-4027-2282-0
ISBN 10: 1-4027-2282-6

For information about custom editions, special sales, premium and
corporate purchases, please contact Sterling Special Sales
Department at 800-805-5489 or specialsales@sterlingpub.com.

CONTENTS

One

THE DREAMING SELF

Who is that spirit that beholds the wonder of dreams?
...In dreams the mind beholds its own immensity

Pippalada, PRASSNA UPANISHAD

When you dream, do you find yourself in exotic places and unusual circumstances—ones perhaps shockingly different from those of your waking life? Do you travel to new and far-away places, do astonishing things, and meet extraordinary people? If so, do not be alarmed, but know that a great many people—if not most people—experience these very same feelings of wonder about the life they find themselves living in their dreams.

Also, be aware that people typically do not dream about the truly satisfactory aspects of themselves, or about relationships that are completely fulfilling and rewarding. So your dreams are more likely to feature things about yourself that are unsatisfactory, incomplete, unfulfilled, and generally in need of attention.

If your relationships are not as good as you would like, you are sure to dream about them in a way that reflects that dissatisfaction; so, too, with sex and intimacy. If your waking sex life does not match your expectations, your dreams will reflect this. It doesn't matter what

sort of lifestyle and what sort of sex life are yours; what matters here is your level of satisfaction. If you are relatively happy and satisfied and consider your life-style and sex life to be in balance, you are unlikely to dream about them.

Looking Inside

Of course, if you are a perfectly balanced person, both psychologically and spiritually, you probably will not dream at all; but then you can be sure that such perfect people do not exist. Many people, however, say, "Oh, I never dream!"—and they really mean it. But oh, yes they do!

They are not being absentminded; intelligent people with the sharpest thinking capacity often claim never to dream, because as soon as they wake, they instantly overrule the dream and discard it as nonsense. Because dreams are "unreal," such people tend to dismiss them without further consideration. So a very clever brain is not necessarily an asset in these circumstances. Indeed, if such people are not careful, they are in danger of living superficially and never looking inside themselves deeply.

You may have noticed this already. Some people don't care to remember trivia, preferring to stick to "real issues." They can even become quite annoyed when friends and colleagues make frivolous jokes. These are the folks least likely to recall their dreams.

Other people—and I admit I am one of these—are likely to remember all the silly things that happen in life and all the nonsense sayings and tend to forget things others regard as earth-shatteringly important. Such people are likely to remember dreams in detail.

Here's a clue about decoding those dreams you do remember. What may seem initially to be utter nonsense may prove to have a very deep meaning! Like almost anything else, the more you practice, the better at it you become—in this case better at remembering all the details of your dreams. Keep a notebook ready by the bed and write down everything you recall of your dream as soon as you awaken, even if it seems silly. The more adept you become at recalling your dreams, the better you'll become at understanding them; and the more you understand your dreams, the better balanced as a person you are likely to become.

Whether you adopt a psychological, religious, or spiritual approach, or merely apply a commonsense and everyday desire to learn, you will certainly agree that we humans are creatures of depth. We all have many layers, and are not confined to what shows on the surface. There's a lot more to us than just that!

So, please, don't just look on the surface of your dreams when you try to decode them. If a dream doesn't seem to relate to anything you already know, it probably has a much deeper meaning. Even if your dream *does* relate to everyday life, don't leave it at that: It will also have deeper meanings hidden inside.

Your dreams may seem ordinary, but you are not ordinary or shallow; you have great hidden depths. If you could look broadly and deeply enough, you would find that everyone is linked in some way. After all, we all live on the same planet, and we must have all descended from the same spark of life.

You might say that Mother Earth herself is constantly working to mold us to perfection, and this is one of her ways of working to bring us closer together and, ultimately, to turn us into one perfect being in tune with the whole of life.

This may sound far-fetched, but it is precisely this type of idea to bear in mind and decipher if we are to understand our dreams fully. I believe that dreams come to us to teach us how to live fuller lives. If we begin to understand them and heed their message, we may achieve the miraculous. It is only our thoughts and anxieties that sometimes prevent us from grasping the lessons to be learned from our dreams.

The Dream Bubble

Imagine yourself floating in space— your "spirit self," shall we say. You have left your physical body behind, sleeping soundly in your bed. Imagine this dreaming psychic self without the skin and bones needed to hold it down. Imagine yourself as a bubble in space—a perfect sphere or a globe floating freely, fluid enough to mold into any shape: Like the surface tension of water forming a hollow bubble, it takes the path of least resistance.

The sun, stars, and planets all form themselves into spheres, complete and whole and alive in their own way. The sphere is a basic shape and very expressive of the wholeness the dreaming self is working to achieve.

So if we want to decode all our dreams and find out why we experience them the way we do, this perfect shape is a good place to start. The sphere or circle can be seen as a *mandala*—a Sanskrit word meaning "magic circle." Even this abstract nonmaterial state of selfhood can be reflected in dreams, as the following example shows:

I seemed to be floating in space, and all around me were orbs like bright bubbles, glowing with different colors that seemed to move and flow like water or oil, like rainbows shimmering, both inside and out. It was all very beautiful and peaceful. Then I became aware of a "black hole," a frightening, dark presence that threatened to swallow up anything in its path. There was no way I could escape, so I just sat or floated there in space. Then the black hole passed over me and disappeared. I still felt perfectly calm and peaceful, because I knew it could not harm me at all.

The basic concept of this dream is interpreted in the last sentence. The dream depicts the feelings of weightlessness, floating, and peace and describes a state of beauty and a lack of physical presence to anchor the dreaming self to the Earth. In waking life we think and feel, which tends to conceal our deeper unconscious and our inner feelings. The hidden inner feelings do not, as a rule, come to our awareness; but they create or select the images that come to us in dreams. These inner feelings, unencumbered by a physical body, can travel where they will and even float freely in space. They can dance in the air and run over the tops of trees and bushes. In dreams we can fly, and often do. It is a common dream experience to have a weightless, flying body as well as a coarse, Earthbound one.

The "black hole" in the dream may have been suggested by something material, something disturbing that was experienced or read about. Perhaps it was the horrific prospect of an actual black hole in space, said to be able to swallow up whole galaxies. But in this dream the dark image demonstrates the truth that materiality has no effect on the transcendental self, and the self is more than the psychological components of the personality which, in our imagination, sometimes seems on the point of devouring the self. This is a very simple dream, but very deep. Often the more spiritual a dream, the more basic its nature. Developing the self by decoding dreams involves much psychological decluttering.

A Magic Circle

The mandala of the self can be visualized as a wheel within a wheel—or perhaps as a sphere within a sphere. The innermost circle represents the everyday self, with the wide-awake experience of awareness toward the top, and the inner feelings (including what Carl Gustav Jung called the *personal unconscious*) toward its base. The larger, encompassing wheel must still be thought of as the self—this time the greater self, including mysterious areas that do not usually seem to be part of ourselves at all. Then, toward the top, we can visualize the human world of spirit—our contact with higher, heavenly matters—while toward the bottom half is the *collective unconscious* (Jung's term again), the source of many of our dream symbols.

These greater contents or principles in the outer wheel are shared equally by the whole of humankind. Taken together, they can be called the *impersonal self*. Neither the human world of spirit nor the collective unconscious is isolated from other people, or from the rest of

A magic circle or mandala may represent the conscious or unconscious self.

creation. There is a constant flow of information taking place among all these different factors that is quite beyond our normal experience. It is from the inner circle of the personal self, with its personal unconscious, that the inner feelings select the images of our everyday or ordinary relationship dreams. In parallel, it is from the greater circle of the impersonal self that the inner feelings are able to select the images for some of our more vivid, meaningful dreams. These are the real or great dreams that we occasionally experience and that contain material from the vast sea of the collective unconscious. In addition, if we are very fortunate, these can also be the truly spiritual dreams deriving from the mysterious world of spirit itself.

The Personal Shadow

In Chinese philosophy the concepts called yin and yang represent the two complementary halves of the globe. *Yang* is the universal principle of the masculine light, the channel through which influences flow, and *yin* the feminine darkness, the receptacle that catches these influences and modifies them, giving rise to new creation. The idea serves to illustrate the principle of the personal shadow of the self. Picture the circle of the self as bathed in light on the upper surface, cloaked in darkness beneath. The division between the two represents the difference between night and day, between waking consciousness and sleep.

During the course of the day, our thoughts and feelings, represented by the objective yang, are constantly assessing everything that comes to their attention. Things they dislike, or find they cannot readily cope with because they are too negative or subjective, tend to be disowned and pushed away. Yet these unwanted contents do not simply disappear;

they sink down into the inner feelings, and may even add to the burden of the personal shadow lurking in the dark depths of the negative yin. We all have a shadow whether we know it or not. Down there, in the darkest part of the hidden side of the personality, is the inscrutable region of the psyche beneath the inner feelings, as though drawn down there by the gravity of materiality. This is the part of the personality that people tend to disown and fail to recognize as their own if it should begin to be apparent. It contains everything pertaining to ourselves that we might think of as undesirable or unlovable, or downright evil. It represents the nighttime Mr. Hyde as the alter ego of the daytime Dr. Jekyll of Robert Louis Stevenson's famous story.

Think of the self—the magic circle of the self—as involving a continual cyclic process. Typically you wake in the morning, go about your daily activities, go to bed, and sleep through the night. All the contents of the psyche are involved in this process, too, as a continuous cycle that works nonstop beneath the level of awareness. In the evening all the activities of the day, experiences, ideas, and emotions—particularly any worries or problems that may have arisen—sink down into the unconscious mind, from the male channel of the yang into the female receptacle of the yin. Down there, in the darkness, they are worked upon, analyzed, and finally reassembled by the inner feelings to emerge in the form of dreams. You may have noticed that the dreams that arrive at dawn, just before you wake, are always the most significant.

You may have learned that seventeenth-century French mathematician and philosopher Rene Descartes actually dreamed the basic principles of analytical geometry and on waking put his inspiration into practice. Similarly, nineteenth-century writer Robert Louis Stevenson said that he used to dream the plots of his novels. *The Strange Case of Dr. Jekyll and Mr. Hyde* (already mentioned as an example of the personal shadow taking tangible form) was the outcome of one of these dreams. Cases such as these of practical, constructive dreams are only well known because they refer to famous people who happened to notice and were prepared to admit the important part dreams had played in their lives; but this type of inspiration, this dream education, is by no means limited to outstanding or exceptionally gifted people. It happens to almost all of us most of the time, whether we are aware of it or not.

The essence and aim of the Chinese system of working with yin and yang is to achieve *Tao*, the path to wholeness, through an even balance of these two opposite but complementary principles. Once some sort of start has been made along this path to wholeness—in our case when the personal shadow has been recognized, and the assimilation of the dark contents of the yin with the bright awareness of the yang has begun to happen—dreams can change their nature. They may warn of the daily need to deal with matters positively as they reach the conscious mind, rather than to follow the old negative habit of pushing them away—*out of sight, out of mind*—into the dark. The following example is a typical dream warning against our misuse of our own personal unconscious mind, perhaps by refusing to accept unpalatable truths:

In my dream there was a hole in the garden, about twelve feet deep and six feet across, into which we had always been accustomed to throw our garbage in the past. I went outside with a piece of old, dirty clothing in my hand and threw it into the pit. There were two men standing by the side of the pit, and they shouted at me crossly: "We've just cleared this pit out, and you are not to throw any more trash into it!" They said I must go down into the pit and clean it out myself. I said I couldn't do that, and felt very alarmed because they were belligerent; and if I went down into the pit, I did not see how I could climb out again. I woke up feeling frightened.

The Hour of Dreaming

When you can remember and start to understand your *personal* dreams, those resulting from the reassembled, re-created, and re-presented impressions of your normal awareness—a second bite of the cherry, which would otherwise not be available to you—then you will begin to experience *impersonal* dreams. You may even receive dream messages from the collective unconscious, showing you deep psychological truths, or from the human world of spirit—the truly meaningful experience of spiritual truths coming to the awareness, things that you ought to know but could not otherwise discover, instructive experiences that will guarantee you are never quite the same person again.

You will find that the nature of dreams varies according to the hour of dreaming or, equally, with your own mental state when you experience the dream. Your personal mandala of the self could be visualized as a clock, divided into day and night.

Your personal sleeping habits may not be typical, of course; but normally, after waking in the morning, by the broad light of noon you will be at your most wide awake. Evening sees you wearied from the day's activities, whether you lead a hectic, busy life or not. Everything that the conscious mind has assimilated, enjoyed, dwelled upon, or pretended not to notice, actively ignored or rejected and disowned—all these impressions are submitted by the now-weary mind into the realm of the unconscious mind. There they become food for the personal unconscious, and this part of your mind—functioning beneath the horizon of awareness—continues to work through the night, throughout your sleeping hours. It is summarizing, comparing, identifying similarities and categorizing them, integrating all your thoughts, feelings, and sensations into a fresh viewpoint, a new understanding.

Dozing dreams—those that appear of an instant as soon as you close your eyes and nod off in your chair—are still in a dissembled state, unintegrated. Because of this, they will seldom make sense when you snap out of your doze and recall them. They will probably bear some semblance to waking thoughts and observations but, jumbled, they will never quite make sense. They are dreams in the making. What is described here is a typically "trivial" evening dream:

There was a row of circular white seats arranged along what seemed to be the ridge of a hill; it might have been overlooking a waterfall. They seemed to be slowly sliding down the rocks at different speeds. I was sitting on one of them, and it was moving faster than the others. It was all very obscure.

On waking, the dozing dreamer was not sure whether the circular objects were really seats after all. They might have been some sticky labels that she had been using during the day. And she was not sure whether anybody else was actually sitting on them or not. So whatever they were, and whatever they represented, this was not even meant to be a dream; it was merely a brief glimpse of the procession of events, memories, and impressions as they passed down into the subconscious—the personal unconscious mind. By itself, the dream picture was meaningless to the conscious mind in whatever way it was interpreted.

Dreams develop and grow as time passes. In the middle of the night—or in the middle, at least, of the sleeping state—remembered dreams tend to be more complicated, indeed more meaningful, but seldom either conclusive or pleasant. By this stage of the dreaming process, the varied impressions they consist of will have been identified and resolved into their true nature, their most appropriate form as products of the weary self: maybe things you would rather not face, worries you have pushed to the back of your mind. Dreams are working toward wholeness, and these matters need to be dealt with. Here they all are in vivid pictorial form: the worries, the fears, and the guilt, all clearly visible. But at this time they represent problems that have not yet been solved, worries that have not yet been put into positive light; they are still in the process of resolution and re-creation.

Consider the following:

I was in a small wood with bluebells and primroses growing among the bushes. I felt I was being followed and looked around in alarm, and saw several mentally disabled men coming after me and quite definitely trying to catch me. The wood now seemed full of thorns and brambles, but I found that I could walk on or run along the tops of these prickly bushes to escape. My husband woke me at this point, as I had been throwing myself about in the bed.

This dream is a typical expression of an unresolved problem, a series of worries or unhelpful attitudes. It seems the dreamer was awakened too soon—otherwise the dream itself probably would not have been remembered. If allowed to continue or recur through the rest of the night, a solution to whatever was troubling the conscious mind of the dreamer may well have emerged, probably toward dawn. In fact, you will find that just before dawn is the time for vivid, truly meaningful dreams to emerge in their completed form. Timed to coincide with waking, they are intended to be remembered. Solution and re-creation, if these are to take place at all with the available material, will by then be complete.

Fear of the unknown, or possibly, as in the last example, fear of mental disorder, or perhaps fear of any kind of stranger: This type of problem is likely to be focused upon and received by way of a dawn dream. To illustrate this, an example of a dream denouncing the folly of racial prejudice is given here. It should be explained that the dream happened during the era of the so-called Cultural Revolution, when, at one time, to most people's bafflement, Chinese nationals in their European embassies sometimes seemed determined to provoke aggressive confrontation with uninvolved and normally completely uninterested passersby. Obviously, this was on the dreamer's mind at the time:

I dreamed of a shadowy Oriental figure, and felt threatened by him. I seized a long pole with a basket tied to the end—the sort of thing that occasionally features in Chinese paintings of peasant life—and began to belabor the shadowy figure about the head with it. Suddenly I saw that he was not Chinese, nor was he at all threatening: He was an elderly Indonesian gentleman (whom I knew in real life and for whom I had the greatest respect). He was laughing at my mistake as he warded off my blows, and I felt dreadfully ashamed of my unreasonable behavior. I felt that I would never again allow myself to misunderstand or prejudge people on the basis of racial differences. This was a dawn dream.

This dream falls into the category *fear of an unknown assailant*—a device often used by the dreaming self to express something that needs facing up to in the dreamer's waking life. In this case the dream was brought to a successful and very worthwhile conclusion: a conclusion that builds character out of chaos, and produces brotherly (or sisterly) love where only fear and suspicion existed before. This, I think, is the very best sort of personal dream.

Two

ANALYZE YOUR OWN DREAMS

There is not a man upon the earth who can interpret the king's dream.

Daniel 2:10

The biblical story about King Nebuchadnezzar's dream in the Book of Daniel illustrates the difficulties involved in trying to decode someone else's dream—far better to discover how to do it for yourself. The king's wise men were unable to explain his dream to him, not least because he wouldn't tell them what it had been about—he expected them to know what it meant anyway! This did not stop Daniel from interpreting the dream successfully, thus saving his own and the other wise men's lives. But then, Daniel did have Divine help. Fortunately you and I—and kings and wise folk alike—can all do better than Nebuchadnezzar by learning how to decode our own dreams.

The Personal Story

Look at your own dream as a story and try to remember everything about it. Think about it carefully; go through the whole sequence in your mind, and write it down with all the details you can remember. Draw a picture of it if you like—you don't have to be an artist. It will help if you list the details separately, in their correct order. Look first at the general story; then read between the lines. Every story has a theme, or more than one theme, to carry it along. Try to recall the theme and the emotions you felt at the time of dreaming and waking.

Your feelings during and immediately after the dream are important pointers. You might remember feeling happy as you experienced one dream detail, sad as you experienced another. You may have felt anxious, annoyed, relieved, worried, pleased, angry, scared, puzzled, or amused; all these feelings are significant if you want to reveal the true meaning of your dream. If more than one emotion is involved, the dream is sure to have more than one meaning: As with all good stories, there will be a deeper meaning hidden within the story line itself. The actual number of meanings a dream may have is unlimited; it all depends how deeply you want to look.

The unconscious mind with its inner feelings—the source of your dreams—uses symbols to get its message across, and symbols can represent more than one thing at once. Their meaning depends on what they mean to *you*, and the deepest meaning is probably the one that has the greatest significance for you. Standard explanations of symbols, such as those listed in Chapter 8 of this book, will be a great help; still, you cannot expect them to tell the whole story.

A personal dream reflects the circumstances that have given rise to it—the things that have happened to you in real life and your reaction to them. If your dream is personal, its contents will be personal, too, and for your eyes and ears alone. Nonpersonal dreams have far greater, wide-ranging meanings—meanings that may have arisen from a collective source. Collective dreams will be filled with more than your own personal contents. As a result, when you experience this type of dream, you will probably be left with no doubt about the meaning. If the dreams seem to be too obscure, the other chapters in this book will help you decode them. Nevertheless, almost all your dreams will relate to you, your own experiences, and your own reactions and often, they will relate to your own deeply considered advice to yourself.

Our minds are miraculously complicated and finely balanced and capable of great things. But our everyday thoughts are not usually the product of the highest part of our minds. We all have similar tendencies: We justify our thoughts, our actions, our attitudes, and our foibles. If we could only use the higher parts of our mind all the time, our reactions and feelings would probably be quite different. It is the higher, or deeper, part of our own self that can let itself be known during the process of remembering dreams.

A Straightforward Message

I have mentioned that dreams have hidden depths, but no matter how complicated the details of your personal dream, the message it carries can be quite straightforward, too—merely expressing some worry that you have put to the back of your mind. Write down the dream story in simple, terms, as in the following example:

In the dream I was upstairs with my brother in (I think it was) our mother's house. I looked out the window and saw two young men acting suspiciously in the garden. One was wearing a mask. My brother said, "Oh, well, they're going to break in, I expect!" and he didn't seem at all worried. In fact, he then went to bed. I was agitated for what seemed some time through the night. I think our mother was in there somewhere, asleep.

Then I heard the break-in I had feared happening downstairs. I could also hear the sound of water running and splashing. I tried to telephone the police, but the operator said: "Sorry, there is a delay. You cannot contact the police for forty minutes." I decided to confront the intruders, and wondered what weapon I could use, but could find nothing suitable.

Then I was downstairs, feeling threatened, and made to sit on the floor against a wall. One of the intruders was carrying a sawlike tool. I was afraid they might torture us. A dog looked in through the doorway briefly, and then went away again. I remember thinking, I don't care what they do to me, but I couldn't stand it if they tortured the dog! (In fact we do not have a dog, and neither does our mother.)

It is a good idea to make out a personal questionnaire. List all the elements of the dream in sequence and, by following your own associations of ideas and your own train of thought, write down (in turn) everything that these details remind you of. Do the same with the themes, if they are at all identifiable. Again, write down anything these secondary elements and themes remind you of, as though following a new story line for each item, until you run out of ideas. When this happens, return to the general picture of your dream and think again. Let your mind spin little incidental stories if you like, but concentrate on the memories that the dream has conjured up.

If you feel that a particular train of thought is becoming too unpleasant to continue, it is best to persevere anyway—you could be approaching something significant that your everyday mind is trying to hide. Even if it shows you in a bad light, no one else will know! It is your own private dream, after all, and intended for you alone. Your personal questions and answers could run something like this:

• *Are you sure it was your mother's house?* I'm fairly sure it was, though there seemed to be no familiar details. I had been on the phone to her during the day, and I had a definite feeling that she was there in the dream.

• *Two men mean anything?* I don't think so. They were skulking about and obviously up to no good.

• *One wearing a mask?* Clearly, he didn't want to be recognized. I don't know why only one of them was masked; he thought he might be recognized, so it could be someone known to us, or probably already known to Mother.

• *Brother went to bed?* He seemed quite unruffled in the dream, but that's how he is in real life! No sense of urgency or danger; too easy-going. It made me feel that it was my own personal responsibility, but it also made me feel quite helpless.

• *Sound of water running?* Mother recently had trouble with the main cistern in the roof, and had to call a neighbor for help. I could have been remembering that. The incident showed that when things go wrong, she has to rely on outsiders, and this can mean loss of security.

• *What about the break-in?* In the dream I was expecting it to happen, and it did. I could hear it happening downstairs. I felt vulnerable but responsible, with no one else available to help.

• *Tried to call the police?* It reminds me of the only time I ever tried to call the police for a real emergency, and the emergency services let me down badly on that occasion. They probably took about forty minutes to arrive.

• *What was the sawlike tool?* It was just an anonymous tool. Mother often has people doing work in the house or the garden. She keeps various tools in the house that used to belong to Father when he was alive, so I suppose there is a security risk there.

• *What about that dog?* I can't make any real sense out of this, except that it stresses how there is no guard-dog protection for the house, and no deterrent for intending intruders. Or perhaps Mother makes us feel a bit like pets ourselves!

• *What were the general themes or feelings during the dream?* First, there was the lack of security and vulnerability; my anxiety and sense of responsibility and helplessness, increased by my brother's complacency.

• *In conclusion:* As we live a hundred miles apart, it is difficult to see what I can do other than keep in touch regularly. This is what I think the dream is telling me to do.

Having completed your questionnaire and answers, look at some of the points again from a nonpersonal angle, looking for other, more cryptic meanings. Try not to rationalize your dream experiences and answers too much; follow them through as though you were listening to a story about someone else. This way you won't try to spare the feelings of the dream characters, and you are less likely to try to spare your own feelings. Don't be too proud to reveal your true feelings for your own scrutiny. Analyze your own answers. Recall your own relationships with the other dream characters—in this case your brother and your mother—especially any unpleasant memories and recent experiences. If you are feeling guilt over some action or neglect on your part, your dreams will work to help you assuage those feelings. Only you can remember your own feelings both during and after the dream: Decide how they fit into the story.

Who is that masked intruder again? Could it be you, the dreamer in disguise, intruding in some other sense? And how about that dog? Could this again be a projection of your own attitude? Your dreams may be revealing the true *you* without your familiar mask or disguise—or they may be portraying you as others are sometimes liable to see you, and you may not recognize yourself. An unfamiliar dog featuring in a dream often symbolizes the dreamer's own hidden self—the shadow—representing those personal characteristics that you have pushed away and refused to face. Your own feelings may have taken the form of a dog to indicate the part of you that does not want to become involved in your mother's problems. The dog in the dream merely looked in and went away again, and you remember that you particularly did not want the dog to get hurt. Could this be because under torture, it might reveal your own secret feelings?

The message of this dream is: Keep in touch with your elderly mother now that she needs some help; visit as often as you can, and when you do, be prepared to help in a practical way.

Breaking The Rules

If you have felt guilty at any stage in your dream, this may be because you have been breaking the rules in real life—your own rules of morality and fair play. This sort of personal rule breaking, denying your conscience, is often at the root of disturbing dreams. The moral is: We all need to be true to our own sense of morality. There is a certain amount of guilt at the back of the next example dream, from a young woman who lives at home with her parents:

I was walking through a large empty building and wanted to go downstairs to go home. Somebody had left a filing cabinet in the way, and that made me feel very cross. I pushed it as I walked past, but it wouldn't move and I nearly fell down an elevator shaft. There was no elevator there, just an open shaft, but this did not seem surprising to me in the dream. I wanted to climb down the shaft, but decided not to. I looked through a window or a hatch in the wall, and saw my boyfriend and my boss laughing and joking together. Then I was at home with my little sister, who was being difficult. She kicked me on the shin and said, "I'll tell Mummy!" A door opened then, and the sound of loud music came through. I opened a window to "let the noise out"; then I heard my father's voice, and he sounded cross.

Your questions and answers could run something like this:

● **What was the empty building?** I think it was supposed to be the place where I work. It felt empty and cheerless in the dream, which is the way I feel about work just now. Things are not going too well, and I recently had a row with the boss.

18

Could this be you, intruding in some other sense?

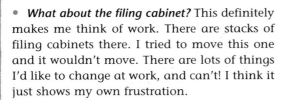

- **What about the filing cabinet?** This definitely makes me think of work. There are stacks of filing cabinets there. I tried to move this one and it wouldn't move. There are lots of things I'd like to change at work, and can't! I think it just shows my own frustration.

- **Why do you suppose it had been left in your way?** It was just typical; everybody has been very difficult and awkward. I suppose I have been acting a bit awkward as well, but nothing seems to go right lately. Since I fell out with the boss, I have been thinking of looking for another job anyway.

- **What did the open shaft represent?** There seemed to be a danger of falling down it and getting hurt. It meant I had to tread carefully. I may have been feeling reckless, but after my row with my boss I was in danger of getting the ax, and perhaps that is what it referred to. It is still a possibility, and I would certainly not like that. If I leave the job, I would rather go voluntarily. I think it was a warning!

- **Why were your boyfriend and your boss together?** My boyfriend is a salesman connected with the same firm. When I told him about my tiff with the boss, he seemed to think it was my own fault, and I felt a bit let down. As I see it, he was siding with the enemy.

- **Kicked by your little sister?** I don't know why she should be acting up. I've done nothing to her to make her feel spiteful. But I was looking after her the other day, and had to stay in when I would rather be going out. There was a bit of a misunderstanding, so when Mother came home she thought I'd been neglectful, but I hadn't. My little sister took advantage of this; she could have spoken up for me, but she didn't. I suppose this is what the kick in the dream meant. Just me feeling badly treated.

- **What about the opening door and the loud music?** I think this followed on from the last incident. The loud music was probably when I went out with a girlfriend and we had a few drinks, and I came back late. I was still feeling fed up. I think the loud music was just me being a bit loud and selfish. My parents were not at all pleased. My father can't stand loud music (though I don't think I have actually played any lately), and he doesn't like me coming home late, either.

- **And the open window?** When I got home, my mother made a remark about me smoking, which she doesn't like, so I opened a window rather sarcastically; I suppose I did it to annoy her. In the dream it got mixed up with the idea of loud music and me being a bit difficult with my parents.

- **The general themes and feelings:** I've been upset so I was feeling at odds with everyone else. I was bad-tempered and a bit rebellious.

- **Conclusion:** It does look as if my private problems at work have been affecting my behavior at home, and my relationship with my parents, family, and friends. I accept that this dream could be dropping me a hint. I need to sort myself out at work and keep cool!

Parts of Yourself

Everything you do finds its way down into your subconscious mind—particularly everything about your relationships that you dislike or cannot understand or that your emotions cannot easily cope with. You may think you have forgotten something, but it has not really been forgotten. It is liable to emerge into awareness again, and the way in which it does this depends upon your own attitude. Ask yourself: Are you basically positive or negative? Do you see yourself as a problem person, or as a growing and developing one—a potentially whole person?

Frightening or disturbing dreams usually point to a problem inside us. If we take note of such dreams and try to understand them, they may help us to face up to and deal with these hidden problems.

When you begin to record and decode your dreams, you will probably meet an opposing influence of some sort, symbolized as an enemy, a villain, a demon, a devil, a witch, a nameless frightener that puts the obstructions in your way. This dark presence is probably a part of your own self, which ought to be released and not contained. Try to identify it and let it come out, if it will. Of course, you may also dream about a very pleasant person who also turns out to be part of yourself. The following dream example includes both these categories:

In my dream I was waiting for my boyfriend, John, to arrive, because I wanted him to meet a special person—a lady who was staying with me, a very sweet person. When John arrived, I rushed to open the door, but in my haste I caused the lady to fall downstairs into the cellar. I shouted at John to go away while I rushed downstairs to help the lady, but John came in. I didn't want him to see what was going on, so I ran back up and tried to stop him going down the stairs. By then the lady had disappeared, but there was something dark and unpleasant down there, and it seemed important to me that John should not see it. He was bringing me some flowers, and I was carrying a vase in my hand, but I wouldn't let him put the flowers in it. He looked down the stairs and said: "What's that down there?" I said, "It's only the boiler!" Then to stop him going down the stairs I grabbed the flowers and started to hit him with them, shouting, "Get out!" I woke up feeling angry and sorry at the same time.

Here are some questions and answers:

- *Waiting for John's arrival?* I felt glad, not because I wanted to see John, but because I wanted him to meet my new lady friend. I thought he would find her attractive and interesting.

- *The lady fell down the stairs?* It was my fault. She was so sweet and harmless, and I knocked her flying when all I wanted to do was introduce her to John.

- *Why did you like the lady so much?* I don't know. She just seemed someone I could admire, and I felt very attached to her. She had a sweet face. I remember now that she had a small mole on her cheek, the same as me. John calls it my beauty spot, and I wanted him to see that, too. Perhaps the lady was just a nice picture of myself after all.

- *Wanting to help the lady?* I felt guilty because they were my private stairs, and I was responsible. No one else was supposed to go down there. It seemed very important for me to get her back again.

- *John came in when you tried to stop him?* I think I was blaming him because the lady disappeared. All I wanted was to get her back up, but John started to come down, too, and this made me angry.

- *What was that dark and unpleasant presence down the stairs?* I can't think what it was, and I didn't really want to see it. I think this was why I was shouting at John, because I didn't want him to see it, either.

- *What about the boiler?* We don't have a hot-water boiler or anything like it in the house, so it wasn't a real one. Come to that, we don't have a basement, either! I remember now that my brother used to annoy me by referring to our mother as "the boiler." It was only fun, of

A vase and flowers are symbols of the persona—how we like to present ourselves to the world.

course: I suppose he meant she was a tough old bird! Perhaps that is where the word came from in the dream. My mother was not in the dream. Perhaps I though that John might think of me as an "old boiler," and I certainly would not like that.

• **Carrying a vase?** I don't know why I wouldn't let John put his flowers in it. It was just that I felt it was my private vase, for me to put things in. I think the vase came from downstairs, and I thought it belonged down there, as though it had something to do with the boiler.

• **Why hit John with the flowers?** I was angry, and then I felt sorry. There was no excuse for doing it in the dream. John had done nothing wrong. It was just temper. I suppose I do have a foul temper sometimes, but I don't want anyone to think of me like that.

• **Themes and feelings:** Up-and-down emotions turning into sheer bad temper. I felt anxious, wanting to present one person and hide another, or keep something unpleasant hidden away from John.

• **Conclusion:** I suppose it means that I want John to see me as a beautiful person and not a bad-tempered tough old bird. Well, who can blame me for that?

Later in the book it will become clear that the last example dream included the personal shadow and the so-called persona—the part of yourself that you would like others to see. The dreamer's bad-tempered shadow personality had to be kept hidden at all costs. The vase she carried was also a symbolic part of her own self—the part of the emotional self that accepts or rejects someone else's advances. In this case she didn't want her friend to pay compliments (in the form of flowers) to her everyday self, but rather to the idealized dream persona that she wanted him to see. Her own anxiety caused this persona to disappear back into the basement of her unconscious mind.

Try not to be too logical about your interpretations. Your logical mind usually wants to keep your own story acceptable to yourself and to the people around you. It is liable to reject anything it considers to be too new, or unknown, or unflattering, or not quite nice. Don't play safe to the extent that you are misled by comfortable but false interpretations. Dreams often involve factors we have ignored or denied while we were awake, and these are the factors, suppressed by our conscious minds, that come to the surface in dreams. These things need to be uncovered, understood, and released from that "basement" if our analysis is to have real value.

When Symbols Keep Recurring

Decoding your dream symbols, provided you are using a reliable book, should be helpful in giving you general ideas to consider, as in the previous example. It is quite common to experience recurrent dreams, involving the same symbols repeating time and time again, dream after dream. Your own inner feelings are giving you a message by way of these recurrent dreams, about some problem that has been affecting your life in an unfortunate way—usually a problem that you don't care to look at or confront in more realistic terms. There are frequently characteristics in ourselves that we don't want to face up to, but should, if we are to become better, more rounded people. If you are experiencing a recurrent dream, start by concentrating on the symbols used by the dream, and try to *feel* the emotions that their memory brings. Your deep, hidden emotions rising from the inner feelings are the source of dream imagery, and you will only understand the dream fully when your outer, everyday emotions are stirred, too. The following is an example of a continually recurring dream experienced by a young woman:

In this recurring dream I am always looking through my closet trying to find something suitable to wear. I know I have to hurry and go out to join in all the activity outside, but I just can't find any clothes that seem right. Everything is too shabby, old-fashioned, brash, or the wrong size. I get very anxious, wondering what to do.

This is a symbol dream that really needs no analysis beyond the simple decoding of the symbol itself. As a dream symbol, clothes represent the way in which we think of ourselves, and the way in which others think of us—or the way we think others think of us. The fact that the dream recurs shows that this dreamer has been lacking in self-confidence. Her own inner feelings are telling her that there is really no need for this. She needs to accept the truth of the symbol. Never mind if her clothes—or her image—are not quite right for the occasion; she is wasting her potential by holding back all the time.

Relationship Dreams

The same symbol can represent a person, a place, a circumstance, an organization, or a principle, presenting an indeterminate number of meanings at one and the same time. As we have already seen, slang expressions can feature as symbols, too—some kind of play on words that, acted out like a TV sketch, make their appearance as real items in your dream. You may have noticed that women's dreams tend to feature collective symbols more commonly than men's dreams. Men tend to build their dreams more around everyday personal experiences, giving them the appearance of real-life incidents; but they are no less dream images for that. They can still be hiding the truth within the fabric of the dream story. Unlike the collective symbols described in Chapter 8, personal dream images will have symbolic validity for you relevant to your own experiences, and they are likely to be known to you alone.

For couples, the subject of relationships tends to give rise to more dreams than any other subject. Within a relationship, dreams can bring out and express the deepest feelings of one partner for the other better than can the conscious, waking self. In a dream both partners' egos will be overruled, to help them see the situation as it really is. We all tend to build up artificial defenses within any relationship involving give-and-take. We have our own habitual little ways of disguising what we really feel, as the following example may show.

A Wife's Dream

There was a tower, and I was peering through an opening into what looked like a dungeon at the base. Inside I could see some dead birds, and I'm not sure what else. My husband was standing behind me, and he asked me what I could see. I peered in again and saw a dead dog in there, so I said: "A dog's body." My husband laughed and said, "We'll soon clear it out!"

Here are the questions and answers:

• **Tall tower?** It was very strongly built. It makes me think of the saying *a tower of strength*, and that makes me think of security, something firm and dependable—rather like marriage is supposed to be, or a family.

- **An opening?** This was simply a convenient hole for me to look into, but various things had gotten in there. They were hidden things, and my husband was asking me what I could see in there. Perhaps he couldn't look in for himself. Perhaps it was only for me to look in.

- **Dungeon?** I did feel in the dream that it was like a dungeon. Naturally, dungeons and towers make me think of being a prisoner, a princess held captive in a fairy tale. But there was no princess in there, only dead creatures and assorted trash.

- **Dead birds?** I suppose the birds had gotten in and couldn't get out again, though there seemed to be nothing to stop them flying out through the hole. Perhaps they had died and fallen down there. Dead birds make me think of lost hopes, lost freedom. Birds are so free to fly about. I remember feeling sad about it.

- **Husband was there?** He was being sympathetic and reassuring about the unpleasant things I could see. He meant well, and he didn't want me to have to look at nasty things. But it seemed that I was the only one who could actually see them. I could only tell him about them.

- **A dog's body?** We have had a dog in the past, but this wasn't any particular one, just an anonymous dead dog—I think—lying among the birds. But in the dream I didn't say, *A dead dog.* I definitely said, "A dog's body," and I thought afterward that this is a slang term for a menial person who does all the work and whom no one cares about. I don't know what this has to do with me, really. We have a loving relationship and we both work hard together to make a go of our business. I hope it doesn't mean that I think I'm taken advantage of. That wouldn't be fair to my husband, who is very sympathetic and caring as well as hardworking. He may not share much of the housework, but he does a lot of other things instead.

- **Themes and feelings:** Frustrated hopes, vague disappointment, a feeling of being trapped and undervalued.

- **Conclusion:** It does seem to have been a picture of our marriage and my doubts, feeling that I was trapped in a lot of hard dull work and the loss of freedom. This aspect of the partnership is a bit disappointing, though I know the business is doing quite well now, and we shall soon be in a much better position. I did marry for richer, for poorer, after all, and I think analyzing and understanding this dream has perked me up a bit and given me some kind of inner strength.

A Husband's Dream

Not all married relationships are quite so well balanced, and many a promising match at the start turns out to be a long-term mismatch, as this example dream shows:

In my dream I was driving a bus with several passengers aboard, including my wife. My wife was being difficult, and kept stopping the bus and getting off, trying to direct it. She tied a rope to the front axle and tried to pull it, and when that didn't work she started pushing it about and rocking it from side to side quite violently. She was holding the journey up and making it difficult for everyone, and I was feeling quite exasperated, though in the dream I was trying to be patient.

The questions and answers:

- **Driving a bus?** I am not really a bus driver, but in the dream it seemed to be my normal job. Everything would have gone smoothly if only my wife would sit down and enjoy the trip instead of making trouble.

- **Wife stopping the bus?** She is never very patient at the best of times, and now she was determined to disrupt the journey. All I wanted was to carry out my job of driving the bus and carrying the passengers safely.

- **She tied a rope to the bus?** I suppose she had to, if she wanted to make the bus go herself, because she can't drive, either in the dream or in real life.

- **Pushing and rocking the bus?** I know my wife couldn't really push a bus about, but in the dream she nearly had it over! It was doing no good at all. The bus was going nowhere, and it was uncomfortable for the passengers. I couldn't see any sense in it, but she was determined.

- **Feeling exasperated?** Of course I was. Nobody was getting anything out of it, she was gaining nothing, and we were getting nowhere. If she wanted to try to drive the bus properly, she could; I wasn't stopping her.

- **The general theme:** Unreasonable behavior, incomprehension, lack of cooperation, clash of desires and responsibilities.

- **Conclusion:** I know it was only a dream bus, but I do like to take my responsibilities fairly seriously. I don't want to be head of the household in particular; I'm not bossy. But having thought about this dream, it seems that my wife feels discontent with the present situation and will not let me persevere with my present course. It all seems to boil down to making a better job of sharing responsibilities.

The dream message seemed to be that their marriage was heading for a breakup, and so it was. When two equally strong-willed people are pulling in opposite directions instead of working together as a team, something is sure to give. They stayed together for a while longer but finally separated, though they are still on friendly terms.

When You Have A Baffling Dream

You can analyze most of your dreams in the way set out in this chapter. But occasionally you will experience a dream that defies analysis—one that seems perhaps to have great urgency and yet no personal meaning, in terms of your own experience. You may be sure that it does in fact have great significance for you—if only you can grasp its meaning! When this happens you may suspect that your own little dream has somehow become superimposed on or mixed up with a much larger, impersonal sort of dream. The ensuing chapters will touch on dreams of this sort.

Three

THE WORLD DREAM

All that we see or seem
Is but a dream within a dream.

Edgar Allan Poe, "A DREAM WITHIN A DREAM"

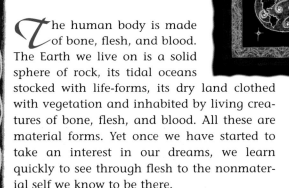

The human body is made of bone, flesh, and blood. The Earth we live on is a solid sphere of rock, its tidal oceans stocked with life-forms, its dry land clothed with vegetation and inhabited by living creatures of bone, flesh, and blood. All these are material forms. Yet once we have started to take an interest in our dreams, we learn quickly to see through flesh to the nonmaterial self we know to be there.

A Voyage of the Mind

We can learn to see through the solid materiality of the world itself. Our dream life will be greatly enriched and our understanding of it greatly enhanced, when we are able to do this. We will become aware of a new dimension in dream awareness when we can see the world of nature itself in the form of a dream—the dreaming state of world consciousness—and express that state as a background to our dreams. When I first began to record my own dreams, this was one of the earliest:

I was looking at bare, stony clay; then I saw that it was a termite's nest, with convoluted tunnels, towers, and shafts; then I saw that it was a great city, with tall buildings and churches, and people hurrying about; then gradually I became aware that it was all a vast sleeping female figure who stirred in her sleep. I knew that this was the great Earth Mother, and that she was dreaming.

This dream expresses a first inkling that solid materiality may not really be quite as solid as it seems. The collective memory of the *great dream* is still part of ourselves at a very deep level, to be recalled occasionally in our own personal dreams. It gives us a glimpse of the natural world in its subtle, nonmaterial state. The trappings of civilization are solid and heavy, and they tend to hold down our inner awareness, which would like to explore such things. We are made to feel somehow guilty for entertaining such abstract thoughts, for even our thoughts seem to cycle around materiality. Most of us think about things rather than ideas—things chasing yet more things endlessly, throughout our lives.

Once we know what it *is*, we can well imagine that in uncivilized days, when people still lived close to nature and manufactured objects were virtually nonexistent, the great world dream was closer to human awareness. The Australian Aborigines still refer to the state of "dreamtime" to explain their origin as a people—their emergence from world consciousness through the mysterious dreaming process of nature.

This imagery used to express these ideas will vary from culture to culture, of course; our dream images tend to relate to our own previous ideas and experiences. But we can all make use of the same principle as an aid to understanding. The whole world can be expressed as a mandala—a cycle of creation. Picture a globe divided horizontally in two. Below this horizon is the dark world of nature, slowly evolving clockwise from bare rocks, through plant and animal life, to human life. Above the horizon all is in bright sunshine. Above the ordinary humans of the world are the "higher humans," saints perhaps, who have left the material world of nature behind. Beyond them in the heart of the mandala is the abode of angels. Beyond them on the right is the realm of archangels, who put the creative cycle in motion—hence the story of the archangel Lucifer, who plunged to earth as the fallen angel.

This is the whole world symbolized in its nonmaterial form. It is our world, and if the personal dreaming self can encompass the whole collective pool of humanity in its imagery—and we have seen, or will soon see, that it can—it can also embrace the whole world in this subtle sense, and experience it as a series of dream images. We are not saints; we are mere humans. All the dark sectors of nature below the horizon play a powerful part in our own innermost being. We are strongly influenced by the animal sector, the plant sector, and especially by the material sector, for it is from this apparently barren world of rocks and minerals that all the wealth of the world is drawn—the force of materiality itself.

What This Means for You

As always, when decoding your dreams, you must remember that a natural cycling process is at work. We have already considered the possibility of personal wholeness—and I believe that our dreams illuminate the slow but steady movement toward that ideal end. The innermost self of most people on earth has been drawn into the world's material zone, attracted by the need for material things—clothes, possessions, money, houses. We should all be experiencing an inward momentum trying to carry our personal psychic center of gravity back from the material to the human zones. The aim of the world dream is to wake up into the light of dawn. There is no way a person can ascend from the material or mineral zones into the bright archangelic zone above them: The cycling movement runs in the opposite direction.

This is actually a symbol of "the way"—the straight and narrow path that world religions teach us about. The only way we can wake from the world dream and come to full awareness of the spiritual world is to pass through the human sector into the saintly sector above it. If you think this is an entirely obscure and abstract piece of reasoning that has nothing to do with your everyday life, you are quite wrong—your dreams can show you things your teachers never taught you because they don't know! The simple act of heeding your dream messages can result in your traveling with the flow of the world dream, rather than following the crowd. The principle often appears in personal dreams, expressed as an alternative course of action or an unpopular choice, as in the following example:

I dreamed I was on a busy street with everybody heading for the bright lights of town. My friends were walking along arm in arm, laughing and joking, and I wanted to join them. Near a store, there was a car parked up off the road, sort of backed against some bushes in the dark. I wanted to tell someone to move the car, as it was in the way. Then I saw that it was concealing an old signpost pointing along a path leading out of town. The path went a very long way through some trees and a park with horses and deer. I heard one of my friends say, "Come on! You don't want to go that way!" But I knew I had to see what was at the end of the path.

On the face of it, the dream certainly did relate personally to the dreamer and her friends, and to her lifestyle, and to the fact that she had been worried about getting into trouble with the law. But the background of her personal dream was the world dream itself. It pointed out the conflict between the things that most people want, with the pleasure they get out of them, and the gentle influence of the world cycle, the counterflowing current of dreams. The dreamer did not actually want to follow that lonely path through the trees, but nevertheless it was something that she felt she ought to do.

Dreams of Climbing

Dream imagery is infinitely variable, and what in one personal dream may be seen as a busy street leading to the bright lights of town may, in another, seem like a direct route to heaven itself. Dreams of climbing up some obstacle, or perhaps a mountain, often express your own burning ambition to succeed, to overcome any difficulties you may have encountered. But at the back of this more obvious meaning, you may again find an image of the great world dream, passing on a message possibly too deep for your waking mind to accept. If in your dream there seems to be a strong element of *wanting* to climb, *wanting* to follow some path, this can be a gentle warning that this particular path is not the right one for you. Through your feelings, your own dream will let you know whether your dream actions reflect a course of life that is running with the world dream, or against it.

The example dream that follows was experienced by an elderly widow who had already dreamed that her late husband was climbing up a steep place—so she assumed—toward heaven. She had been trying to reestablish contact with him in one way or another, and this was the lesson taught by the dream: Don't do it! Her conscious aim, indeed her ambition, had been to rejoin her husband by following him on the climb, but when this sort of decision is made deliberately, as the world dream implies, it is more likely to lead the wrong way—to the rocky heights of materiality. The world dream teaches us that the only dream climb that can be truly rewarding on a long-term basis follows the direction of the natural cycle, leading from the state of materiality where most people live (and rightly so, because we cannot manage without material benefits) back through the dark world of nature to the point of human birth, or rebirth.

At the start of this dream I found myself with very many more people, going along a high ridge, so narrow that we had to crawl in case we fell off. We seemed to be creeping along the knife-edged top of a mountain ridge. We could just see that on one side it was grass-covered and almost perpendicular. We couldn't see the other side, as it seemed to be straight down from underneath the narrow path. Gradually the people in front of me seemed to have disappeared, and I was in the lead. I went carefully on, and then realized there was no longer a grassy side. In fact, there was nothing under the path where I was. I could see that a tremendously long way down there was a sort of very pleasant-looking parkland, with people walking about. The path I was on came to an abrupt end. It was impossible for me to turn around, so I started to edge my way backward. This was very difficult and nerve-racking. At last I caught a glimpse of grass, but as I looked it just seemed to move farther back. This happened again and again. I got into such a panic that it woke me up.

Decoding a Mysterious Truth

If your dreams are advising you to set your sights in a certain direction, and swim with the tide, can you avoid trying to travel in the wrong direction? Certainly! You simply need to remember your dreams and accept their message. Whether you are a religious person or not, remember that there is a greater will than your own, and agree inside yourself to be carried along by that will. Your hopes will then be realized in the very best way, because you will be in harmony with the world dream, and thereby with the whole of creation.

Picture the world mandala again, with its division between the dark world of nature and the bright spiritual zone above it. The upper part represents world consciousness; the lower part represents the world dream. It may be a feat of the imagination, but it reflects the true picture quite accurately. Creatures of nature (and in this sense they include us) are quite unaware of world consciousness, or the bright dome of spirituality above them. Nature is the world's sleeping and dreaming process at work. In this sense, along with the lives of animals, plants, and even rocks and minerals, mountains and rivers, we are all merely dreams of the nonmaterial world—of the great Earth Mother herself.

The cycle of creation includes the great fall, and this is a most important symbol—the archangel who fell from heaven to earth to rule over the world of materiality. The sensation of falling often features in unpleasant dreams, and usually occurs at the evening end of the night, soon after falling asleep. The dream itself will very likely have a counterpart, some sort of related experience of insecurity in waking life that triggered the dream, and which can be analyzed by the dreamer. But this is likely to be its root: the great fall mirrored from the world dream, a plunge from light to darkness. There are many forms, but this example is perhaps typical, featuring a vague sense of disregarding advice from a higher authority:

I was on the battlements of a church tower, and decided to climb up to the top of a pinnacle to see the view from there. I felt perfectly safe. Then a robed figure like a bishop came clambering up the wall toward me and said, "It's not safe, and there are some alterations due!" But I said, "Never mind about that!" And then next thing I knew I had slipped and was falling in a panic. I woke up in a sweat before I hit the ground.

Dawn Dreams of the World

The sensation of falling is related to the thoughts and impressions of the day passing down into the subconscious mind at night, but in cases like this, the dream portrays it on a world scale. This vast unconscious mind of the world, formulating the impressions gathered during its spiritual day, collates and develops them by way of the growth of plants rooted in the soil, through the mobile and more actively conscious lives of the animals, through the yet more conscious but still dark and primitive stirrings of humanity. It passes through the entire gamut of the natural world, finally arriving at lucid awareness in the sunrise of the whole assimilated human self. This is the perfect outcome of the world dream: the evolution of nature, culminating in the perfection of the human psyche. It is only by way of the dawn dreams of the world that we as human beings might one day come to whole awareness—the perfect consequence of materiality.

The world mandala covers our own personal lives as well as the collective life of the planet, and the sectors within the world of nature can equally be seen as sectors of our nature: a human part, an animal part, a plant part, and a material part. Of these, the material part is the most solid and tangible—not merely our material bodies (for of course we are all material objects in that sense), but our psychic contents as well—the subtle, world dream nature of materiality.

Material Foundation of Dreams

Materiality includes the force of gravity, magnetic fields, and all the laws of physics. Gravity has a need, so to speak, to gather everything into the deepest, heaviest part of itself, and hold it all together; a black hole in space has this nature. When translated into human terms, the concept of materiality means the desire to possess things, to have and to hold. This essential foundation for human life is a constantly recurring background of our dreams:

In my dream I was in a place like the Grand Canyon, or an enormous quarry. There were miners or quarrymen far below me, digging out heavy metal and carrying it along the bottom of the canyon toward some factories. Factory smoke was blowing up the canyon. I was going to climb down when I met my family sitting on some rocks. They were moving their heads and talking and smiling at me, but then I saw that their bodies seemed to be made of stone growing out of the ground. There were lots of very pretty little stones piled up round about. I looked at some of these stones admiringly. Then Mother got up and said: "Don't they look nice? But there's never enough of them!" She closed the door, and I saw that we were in our house.

This seemed to have been an incompletely formulated dream, remembered when the dreamer woke up during the night after sleeping for an hour or two. It expresses how completely dependent we are on the material instinct. Even our own body is a material object, and we could not live without it. It ensures that everything falls into place and functions correctly, according to physical laws. But there is not really any sense of altruism in it, of helping or caring. When children grow into adults, they become filled with this type of instinct, and feel the need to acquire all sorts of things for themselves—money, houses, other people as partners or children or employees, consumer goods of all sorts, all the good things of life. Nobody is to blame for this; we live in a material world, and it is good to share in its bounty.

In Harmony With the World Dream

～～Some dreams illustrate the dreamer's inner progress, when the dreamer does seem to be living in harmony with the steady cycle of the world dream. Some people's dream imagery habitually corresponds with the nature categories of the world mandala more closely than others—progressing from the mineral, to the plant, to the animal, and to the human sectors.

> *I was walking in the dark but carrying the kind of light I use at work—an electric lightbulb on a long cord trailing behind me. I was walking along a path with bushy, overgrown vegetation on either side. Then I came to an open field, and I felt the plug jerk out of its socket, and the light went out. There were sheep in the field, and I walked among them in the dark. Then the path came to a place where I couldn't go any farther, and I stopped. But looking ahead, I saw myself still walking on, along a road illuminated by streetlights.*

This dream very clearly expresses the progress of the dreamer's life journey, running with the flow of the world dream. Plants are rooted in the earth. In effect, the dreamer within any sector has something of the inner nature of that sector: the individual whose psychic center of gravity is within the plant sector is also still rooted—still dependent upon and closely attached to materiality. The light becoming unplugged as the dreamer left the bush vegetation and reached the open field where the sheep were grazing suggests that this psychic connection with the material force had been severed. The dreamer's psyche, by way of the inner feelings, moves through the animal sector, and on reaching its limits—the dreamer's current position in life—is still able

to see ahead, to see the future self on the human road.

In Chapter 1 we saw that personal dreams may change their nature according to the hour of dreaming—depending on how developed the dream process is in the individual's sleep. The same applies to individual dreams based on the world dream, because the life of plants and animals contains something of the nature of the personal shadow, on a grand scale. The contents of this world shadow are liable to emerge in the form of an unexpected adversary or a hidden danger. On the face of it, we may expect some animals to behave in a dangerous manner; at first sight, however, plants do not seem particularly threatening, or likely to frighten anyone— until we take a world-scale view of their fiercely competitive lives.

The Secret Life of Plants

～～From a plant's point of view, humans seem to live their lives at a frantic pace. From the human point of view, plants seem to live their lives in slow motion; but they, too, have instinctive movements, triggered by light, gravity, moisture, air, and the need to feed. Speeded up, we would see that plants are constantly on the alert, waging war with each other, struggling to the death without letup, as the following example suggests:

> *In my dream I was walking in a dense forest with sunlight filtering through the tops of the trees. Everything near the ground was dark and mysterious. Instead of green, everything seemed to be red, or black, but this did not seem at all unusual in the dream. The ground was sticky as though saturated with blood. All around I could sense great danger lurking in the darkness, and I seemed to feel rather than hear a great roaring and shrieking. The tension seemed unbearable. I knew there was a way out of this forest not far*

away, where everything would be much safer, and I tried to press on toward it, but felt as if I was rooted to the spot, and could move only very slowly, as if wading through treacle. Perhaps it was the blood holding me back.

If the dreamer could have analyzed his own dream, he would probably have given it a personal interpretation. He had felt trapped in his own turbulent thoughts, and desperately needed a way out of his problems; but this does not alter the fact that the images are on a world scale, tapped directly from the unconscious mind of the world itself.

So, from the viewpoint of the world dream, the woods are not so peaceful a place as they seem: They are gory battlefields, filled with the victorious, the defeated, the dead, and the dying. Ancient forests may seem stable communities, but only because all the members are constantly vigilant with their neighbors, defending the place they have won. You will see that dreams dominated by the plant sector of the world's unconscious mind will tend to have the nature of aggressive competition, ruthlessness, or the will to power.

The Secret Life of Animals

Frequently involving pride, wariness, and sexual desire, dreams using symbolism relating to the secret world of animals can carry important lessons regarding social interaction. Moral boundaries are often a matter for the animal nature rather than for the human nature. Animals normally maintain strict rules governing their own behavior and do not care to breach them. This is basic morality—being true to their own instinctive barriers and boundaries.

Rules are important to the unconscious mind, and breaches of these rules are frequently at the root of adversarial dreams. Such dreams probably will not involve ani-mals at all. However, I often hear about dreams in which the dreamer seems actually to be an animal, involved in specific animal pursuits. These dreams, too, may carry a personal message for the dreamer when analyzed; but taken at their face value alone, they can offer an intriguing view of instinctive animal life. The dream that follows was in fact analyzed in terms of everyday life, and did have something important to say to the dreamer about her family relationships, but it can also be seen simply as a traumatic incident in the life of a fox!

In the dream I was a fox—a vixen—and I was searching around trying to find my cubs, when I saw sitting in some very long grass a large dog fox that I was afraid of and very anxious to escape from. So I jumped a nearby hedge on the road and crossed to the other side, then went down the road for a short distance, then started to cross back again. About halfway over, a large bus came speeding around the bend above me. I only just had time to reach the side and jump the hedge. This time I got caught up for a moment in the hedge—there might have been barbed wire there—and when I tore myself free it hurt my leg quite badly.

The Human Element

Moral boundaries can more easily become blurred in the world of humans than in the corresponding worlds of plants, animals, and things. This is because humans are freer than the lower creatures of nature—we have choice, which they lack. People seldom dream directly about their psychic qualities or their spiritual level in the world, unless they are currently changing—when they have risen to a more evolved position in life, or are in danger of sinking to a lower one. To dream that you have left a lower condition and reached a higher one is always good news, although its message may be disguised:

I was on a chain bridge over a river, looking back at some jungle type of forest full of fierce animals. The animals could not walk on the chains, so I was safe. There were creatures in the river, too, but they could not survive out of the water. I was quite relieved to cross the river and reach a village. A friendly dog ran to greet me, but then I saw it wasn't a dog, but a boy I knew. I said, "I thought you were a dog," and he laughed. Then I was in a marketplace, full of people and stalls with meat and vegetables, and birds in cages. The people were a very mixed bunch: white, black, Chinese, and Arabs, and lots of children.

The dreamer had been going through a sticky patch at work, and felt very deeply that it was "a jungle out there"! Wild animals seemed an apt simile for his colleagues, clients, and nagging employers, and he had decided to leave his job to try self-employment in the travel industry. Naturally, it had been a worrying time for him, and the future still seemed uncertain. But when the world dream reference was pointed out to him, his self-esteem and confidence received a much-needed boost, for the dream was telling him that his human status had been improved. When we remember our dreams and submit to the world dream at their root, the real-life move from employment to self-employment is a step that fits our newfound independence and freedom of choice. It represents one aspect of the symbolic state of wholeness toward which our dreams seem to be working.

Four

DREAMS AND PSYCHOANALYSIS

If we meditate on a dream sufficiently long and thoroughly—if we take it about with us and turn it over and over—something almost always comes of it.

C. G. Jung, AIMS OF PHSYCHOTHERAPY

We have much for which to thank the big three psychotherapists—Sigmund Freud, Alfred Adler, and C. G. Jung—when it comes to their combined work on bringing to light our hidden psychic depths. As Freud pointed out, "The interpretation of dreams is the royal road to knowledge of the unconscious activities of the mind."

But we might be excused for thinking that Freud seemed to be somewhat obsessed with sex: He saw dreams largely as an expression of repressed sexual desire. The sexual element, he claimed, was often so distorted by the dreaming process that it was no longer recognizable as such. It was this distortion, he claimed, that represented the resistance set up within the self to prevent conscious exploration of the unconscious mind. "We desire most that which is forbidden," he said. Since sexual desires during Freud's lifetime were the most taboo factors in society, they were the factors that tended to become repressed. Repressed sexual desire, he claimed, was the chief factor at work in the subconscious from early childhood on, forming people's character and molding their behavior.

Royal Road to the Unconscious

Freud believed that the psyche includes a built-in censor, the function of which is to disguise the form of anything the conscious mind finds distasteful. He termed this *the endo-psychic censor*, visualizing it as a psychic force able to modify anything incompatible with the dreamer's conscious self-opinion. In effect, it is able to produce a cartoon picture out of a real situation, making it less offensive and more acceptable to the waking mind. You can understand the significance of a political cartoon in the newspaper—or the real message of a dream—only if you know something about the people and events to which it refers. Without this inside knowledge, it will be merely an amusing drawing.

Freud divided the actual contents of the dream into two types: the manifest, and the latent. *Manifest content* sets the scene with details taken from the dreamer's own waking experiences. *Latent content* is the plot of the play—the cryptic political message of the cartoon, and the true meaning of the dream. Some would say that the following example is a typically "Freudian" dream, and possibly rather typical, too, of the times a century ago:

I dreamed that my friend gave me a present of a beautiful ivory carving, and it seemed extremely precious to me. I placed it reverentially in a jeweled wooden casket and carried it into the cathedral, where I placed it on the altar. I saw one of the clergymen then, and asked him if it would be all right, but he just looked at me oddly and walked away without speaking.

Freud would, I am sure, have seen this as a sexual dream. The young man who dreamed it, Freud would have said, had a clandestine crush on his friend and, in view of the restrictive inhibitions of the age and his own deep feelings of guilt, was expressing through the dream his wish to make the relationship acceptable both to his sense of morality and to the world in general.

The Will to Power

Where Freud put the psychic emphasis on sexual impulses, Adler put it on an inner drive for power. He saw the inherent need for self-assertion as the basic motivation of people in general, and of young people in particular. Both Freud and Adler were agreed that if the great reservoir of repressed mat-

erial stored within the unconscious could be recovered and reintegrated by the conscious mind, the individual would be better adjusted as a person.

But where Freud saw sexual desire as the main substance of repressed material, Adler identified the drive for power as the most important factor. Adler maintained that children in particular are bound to suffer from feelings of inadequacy during their first few years of life, being small, weak, and uninformed; he saw the resultant inferiority complex as the common root of personality defects. Everyone, he argued, possessed a will to power, and if this will was frustrated, the individual was bound to look for ways in which the balance could be redressed. If personal accomplishments were not enough to achieve coveted self-confidence, the individual would fall back on fantasy. Feelings of inferiority cried out for compensation, he said, and this basic drive was reflected in our dreams, too. The warnings and encouragements transmitted by dreams were aimed at showing us how to surmount the obstacles that stood in the way of our personal supremacy.

New Growth in the Desert

So Adler saw the craving for power and status as the basic, if hidden, obsession that influenced our lives from early childhood on. Power was the dominant theme during the first five years of life; but soon after that, puberty began and sex became the dominant theme. In this regard, we could say that power progressed to sex, that Adler's system gave way to Freud's, as though part of a natural, cyclic process.

If we set this idea against the world mandala—the world dream—the pattern reveals itself. From the spiritual lifelessness of the material zone, the psychoanalytic movement sets the cycle in motion. Dreams are not merely manifestations of our repressed sexuality and our cravings for power; they match the inner workings of the world dream itself. From barren rock and desert, plants eventually grow, seeking power as a first priority to claim their own piece of desert. The following example is a typically Adlerian dream:

I seemed to be struggling through a deserted, barren place without sign of life. There was plenty of abandoned garbage. There were old cars, fuel drums, and builders' debris. Apart from these, it was like the Sahara, with loose sand difficult to walk in. I felt uncomfortable and weak. Then I came up to a huge stone wall. It seemed to be a fort, the type you might see in films about the French Foreign Legion or the Crusades, and I tried to get inside. There did not seem to be any way I could get in or climb up the wall. There were a few people on the battlements walking past and ignoring me, and I started to shout and wail. Some of them glanced down at me with contempt and then went about their business. I felt very small and helpless.

This was the dream of a man who had been going through a difficult time at work. He thought of himself as ambitious, but could not seem to progress or make any impression on his employer. He did not get on very well with his colleagues, and felt that his employer was a bully who wanted to keep him in a menial position, and would not give him the chance he deserved. The dream fits into the world mandala in this context: To a plant, a lifeless desert represents an utter lack of power. There would seem to be no reason, in terms of space and opportunity, why a person—or a plant—should not succeed without limits, and yet it does not and cannot happen. The situation is barren and hopeless, and seems little better than death.

A Collective Intelligence

Freud takes his place in the animal sector of the world dream. Sex, for him, is at the heart of everything, and without it no creature could exist. Adler takes his place in the plant zone of personal power. Jung moves to the human sector, aiming toward psychic completion.

The world dream drops the hint that all seemingly human dreams originating below Jung's point of entry are less than truly human. Even though the dream imagery will take human form, it will have the essence of plants, or of animals. Dreams that fall in the material category are in the majority. But dreams, like people, need to progress, to mature, and to follow the subtle movement of the world dream. Only truly human dreams relate to the collective unconscious, which is filled only with nonmaterial images, not of nature but of humanity. Spiritual dreams start here, too, for the human world of spirit is intimately connected with the sea of the collective unconscious. Only when our ordinary dreams become *great dreams*—when they come under the supervision of the collective intelligence—will they contain material from beyond our waking experience. Truly human dreams may be selected at this deep level in order to involve and inform other individuals as well as the dreamer: a universal endo-psychic center capable of guiding us all.

Archetypes of the Collective Unconscious

Jung was powerfully aware of this collective dimension in a way that Freud and Adler were not. Jung could see a tendency

A bearded man with a kind face may symbolize Dionysus, who could foresee the future.

common to all, enabling modern people to understand life in a manner psychologically conditioned by human history—a tendency he called archetypal. *Archetypes*, he said, were shared forms of perception that probably existed even before the development of consciousness as we know it: inborn conditions of intuition, or primordial images that could take the form of unquestioned emotional certainties or of dream images. They reached the surface of awareness notably on important occasions: birth, death, danger, triumph, defeat, changes of psychological orientation such as puberty, or any unfamiliar, awe-inspiring, or frightening experience. Unconsciously, when such things occurred, we used the imagery of our ancient ancestors—those ancients who were not yet familiar with the world of materiality; people who in spiritual terms were still close to their own innocent childhood.

The most common archetypes include the *anima*, or female soul, in men, and the *animus*, or male soul, in women. These enable the two sexes to understand intuitively the other's very different points of view. The understanding inherent in these archetypes help men be empathetic and women assertive. Other archetypes include the kind old wise person—who always has good advice to offer—and the great Earth Mother, or goddess, who can provide similar (if more earthy) advice. Then there is the *persona*—the social mask people tend to wear—and the shadow, which takes an unlimited variety of forms and with which we are already familiar. Finally there is the self, often seen as an innocent child observing the world. The body of these figures may be formed, or filled in, by the dreamer's own life experiences, but their essence is primordial and archetypal.

Ancient Myths

Jung claimed that in dreams, people often experience archetypal symbols to be found in the myths of ancient civilizations—matters about which they had no previous knowledge. While pointing out these features, he believed we should try to work things out for ourselves, finding the meaning of our own dreams. He encouraged the people who consulted him to draw or paint their own dreams, recording them like an illustrated story, to bring out the symbolism while the memory was still fresh. This is still an excellent exercise and will encourage further meaningful dreams to present themselves. To portray your dreams sets the self on a course sympathetic with the world dream. The following dream is "Jungian." Though simple, it is full of ancient symbolism:

I was walking through a forest and came upon a sunlit glade, in the middle of which was an old stone column with a sundial on top. I went up to it, and saw that it had writing on it that said TIME IS JOY. There was something like a banked ditch all around the sundial, with ivy growing in and along it. I parted the ivy with my hands and looked through it and glimpsed ancient ruins and carved stones. In the ditch, it seemed I could see to a great depth with many different layers, and there were people and horned animals of some sort. Then I saw nuts rolling on the ground, and looked up to see, standing by the sundial, a tall bearded man wearing a robe. He had a kind, gentle face, and was carrying a baby who was chuckling and holding out a nut.

Jung might have pointed out connections with ancient myths in this dream. Ivy, as well as the vine, is a symbol of Bacchus, or of Dionysus, a god who belongs equally to the world below and the world above. He has often been represented in myth as a robed, bearded man with a kind face. Dionysus was identified with Faunus, and with Pan, and with Silvanus, all spirits of the forest who let the future become known in dreams. He was also identified with Kronos, the god of time and change.

This ambivalent figure can also represent the dreamer's archetypal father figure, or a wise old man who can see the future. The chuckling child was none other than the dreamer's own self, being carried willingly along by this kind and gentle power. Nuts in ancient times were used as children's playthings, or as pieces in various games—but nuts are also full of hidden meanings. They can represent the head with its concealed thoughts, or potential growth hidden in the future—the eventual fruition of the forest of the mind. The celebrations over which these gods of growth presided, involving horned animals, were joyful occasions, something in the nature of a present-day harvest festival. The stone column of the sundial, by its phallic shape, represents generative power; the sundial itself is a personal mandala, with everything that such a symbol entails. All these themes are interlinked and express the renewed workings of an ancient process of personal fulfillment.

Five

SHARING YOUR DREAMS

Let's consider who it was that dreamed it all...
It must have been either me or the Red King. He was part of my dream,
of course—but then I was part of his dream, too.

Lewis Carroll, THROUGH THE LOOKING GLASS

If you like the idea of sharing your dreams and their interpretations, it may be right for you to seek out fellow dreamers who will help you to unravel your dreams and reach a constructive conclusion. Bear in mind, however, that dreams sometimes contain hidden layers of meaning; when decoded, these may reveal unpleasant or unflattering matters that many people find too personal, maybe even too embarrassing to share. Your psychic underwear may be pulled out of the laundry basket and spread out for all to see and gossip about. If you do not like the idea of this possibility, I suggest that the do-it-yourself method is best for you.

Dirty Linen

Not a few people, though, simply love to wash their dirty linen in public, and to discuss their emotional and sexual problems in detail. Some of the free-and-easy audience-participation shows on TV will bear this out.

Who's to say who is right? If you like to talk about yourself—and if so you will certainly be in the majority—well, why not? And why should others not get to hear about it? Understanding your dreams on a shared basis will do much to allay emotions that are flying out of control. The fact that you are sharing your problems can reassure your worried mind and ease relationships that have become strained. Your social life will probably become more pleasant as a result.

Sharing your dreams with others will help you look inside your own mind, to discover and assimilate your own brand of hidden wisdom and find your own key. You may have been baffled by a dream—perhaps because it was confusingly complicated, or possibly because it was misleadingly simple. Allowing someone else to prompt your thoughts with a few appropriate questions will often help. Another person may introduce a viewpoint that had not occurred to you; you will have found a new stance, a new way of looking at an old problem. The guided conclusion of the following example dream was an eye-opener for the young man who dreamed it:

In my dream I had gone to visit the old home. It was a large mansion that had seen better times, and had plainly been neglected for many years because it looked on the point of falling down. It had gables and ornate little towers that looked unsafe. It had slate missing off the roof, the porches were crumbling, the woodwork was rotted, and the staircases were rickety; all the plaster was falling away, the windows were broken and the shutters hanging loose on their hinges. I had intended going back to stay for a while, but as it was plainly an uninhabitable ruin, I did not go inside.

Instead of your personal questionnaire, it will now be others who, using their experience of decoding their own dreams, will ask the questions:

• **Do you really live in a mansion?** No, I live in a very ordinary house. I've never really lived anywhere like that dream mansion.

• **But in the dream you thought of it as home?** It seemed to be the place where I used to live. I don't know why. It would have been a great place for kids to grow up in, I suppose. But nobody could live there when it was falling down like that.

• **The personal self is often symbolized in dreams as a building. Any ideas?** I don't feel that it was meant to be me personally.

• **Have you recently been in touch with anyone else?** Well, yes: I visited my mother in the hospital.

• **What were your feelings toward her?** Well, obviously, I was concerned about her; a bit anxious.

• **Could it be that you were overconcerned, over-attached?** Well, yes—I suppose I was feeling rather like a dependent child again!

Passive and Active Roles

This last example described a completely passive dream in which the dreamer did nothing except observe the old house, and yet it contained a hidden psychological truth. The dreamer realized that he had been tied to his mother's apron strings to some extent, and he saw that his mother's "house" had been a fine place for him to live as a child, but the time had come to adopt a more adult attitude toward her. The assimilation of this dream really made a big difference and set the individual concerned on a new course through life.

When you first start remembering and recording your dreams, your own role in them does tend to be passive—you are merely watching while the dream takes place before your sleeping eyes. But as time goes by, your dreaming self tends to take a more active part in the dream. Instead of remaining a member of the audience, you will have become an actor, playing your own role, acting and reacting with the other dream characters. The way we act in our dreams, whether in an active or passive role, reflects the way we are liable to behave in real life. Assimilating the message of your own dreams can have a positive effect on the sort of person you are.

Being passive is not quite the same as possessing a gentle nature. It sometimes happens that people who live very quiet, inoffensive lives find themselves dreaming violent dreams, full of aggression and passion. Or the situation may be reversed: A person who is hyperactive in real life may experience dreams of peace and beauty, and restful pursuits. This is only to be expected, as your dream life works toward wholeness and balance. Ideally we should all possess an even balance between action and inaction. We should be assertive when the situation calls for control, submissive when matters cannot be controlled and must therefore be tolerated. *Balancing dreams* are often concerned with morality: Excessively moral people may dream of letting their hair down; wild ones may dream of piety and prudence. Discussing your dreams with fellow dreamers may help to make these issues clear, by pointing out inner discrepancies and balancing the outer personality.

Seeking Compensation

Sexual compensation is sometimes demanded by the physical body when deprived of its natural functions. This may emerge by way of the inner feelings, in exaggerated imagery experienced in your dreams. Dream sex may be making a point to the conscious mind, indicating that repression is taking place, or that resentment for some reason is building up to reinforce the personal shadow. Unlike the everyday emotions, the inner feelings are able to take the long-term view; better to shock the waking conscience than to create a monster in the unseen depths of the subconscious mind. The following example came as a shock to the dreamer, a married woman with a fairly typical marriage:

I dreamed that I was lying in bed, having sex with my husband's business partner, and was just reaching a glorious climax when my husband came into the room. I nodded and smiled at him, and he started to walk up to me, but I think there were some crocodiles in a swamp at the side of the bed, and I warned him not to step on them and stir them up, as they might be dangerous! There was a squirrel sitting on one crocodile's back, and it sprang onto the bedrail chattering. Then I woke up, feeling quite elated.

Through various questions and answers, the other dreamers in her group helped her to arrive at a satisfying conclusion, though it did little to ease her long-term feeling of frustration:

• *Pardon us for asking, but have you had sex with your husband's business partner?* Certainly not! I don't even like him very much.

• *In your dream, when your husband walked in and caught you both at it, what were his reactions?* He just looked blank, as though he weren't involved.

• *There were crocodiles in the dream. Monsters like this are supposed to represent dormant passions.* Well, I can be quite passionate when I want to be! In the dream I was a bit concerned in case they ate him.

• *And a squirrel was involved, too. What are your thoughts on squirrels?* I think they are friendly and playful—though I know somebody who got bitten by one when she was trying to feed it.

• *Perhaps there is a "monster" and a "squirrel" in your life. How is your sex life as a rule?* Fine, as far as it goes. But my husband works long hours, and he's often too tired—or so he says.

• *Do you think he's being unfaithful to you?* He'd better not be! I would walk out.

• *Well, how do you feel about your marriage?* It's just that I sometimes feel married to the business; I think he should spend more time at home. I wouldn't really be unfaithful to him. I felt a bit guilty after I woke up and started thinking about the dream—but why should I feel guilty? I've done nothing wrong. I think the dream was just teaching him a lesson in my imagination for neglecting me.

A Touch of Guilt

The personal unconscious is the natural home of morality and law-abiding behavior. Our conscious minds may allow us to do things that we would certainly refrain from doing if someone in authority were watching—breaking the rules in small ways. On the surface we may think this is perfectly acceptable, if we can get away with it. But under the surface of consciousness we can get very upset by this sort of behavior, without even realizing it! This state of affairs features quite often in dreams, and it may need a few gentle questions to uncover the truth. The result—if it is accepted—will be a better-balanced psyche.

I was in a sort of room lined with hundreds of different shapes of all different hues. There was a narrow space between some sort of cupboards, with some people outside. To show them how easily I could get through this narrow gap, I held my arms above my head and sort of danced through. Then I saw that I had touched the sides, and picked up a nasty stain on my blouse.

The dreamer thought later that the room in the dream might have been just a store. She had certainly been shopping the previous day, and this may well have triggered the dream. Such triggering events frequently provide a clue to decoding your dream. Her fellow dreamers followed up this lead:

• *What did you buy, anything special?* No, just normal day-to-day groceries.

• *A stain on clothes usually implies some sort of guilty feeling. In this case, something connected with shopping?* At first the dreamer could not think of anything; then she said: "Well, I did get too much change when in a store a couple of weeks ago—but I didn't notice until after I'd left the store anyway."

It may have been a small matter, but that was most likely the message of the dream: Be honest in small things! These things matter to the inner feelings and upset our psychic balance. If you do share your dreams with others, and find yourself not telling them something that may be connected, but which makes you feel uncomfortable, think about it very carefully! Most likely, this is the whole point of the dream. It is always advisable to write down your dream as soon as you wake, if it helps you to remember it. But resist the temptation to embroider the details, to alter the fabric slightly to make it seem more interesting, or to show yourself in a better light. You are more likely to give way to this temptation if you are sharing your dreams with others. Make sure the details you give are the true facts!

Whether you do share them or not, make a point of recalling and writing down any real-life events that you think could be even vaguely connected with the subject matter of the dream. Your inner feelings recognize associations with past events, and may be using them to tell you something. Some long-repressed emotional hurt that would be better aired and resolved—this is the type of thing at the root of dreams, triggered by recent incidents and categorized as similar by the unconscious mind. Remember to pay particular heed when you have a vivid dream.

Reentering Your Dream

If a dream seems to you to have been unfinished, as though an important conclusion has been lost by waking up too soon, try to reenter and reexperience it. You need to sit somewhere quietly, make yourself comfortable, and close your eyes—but don't go into full sleep. Recall your dream gently without trying to think about it. Imagine you are watching a rerun of the dream; simply reenter it and let the sequence run by itself. You should be able to reexperience the dreaming state without actually sleeping. Follow the dream step by step; let it run on past its previous conclusion. As you are not really asleep, you cannot really wake up when the dream is apparently finished; allow it to continue until it reaches a satisfactory conclusion. Avoid deliberately inventing incidents or solutions— allow the sequence to unfold itself naturally. If you have someone else on hand to help, you can describe to your companion what is happening in your reentered dream. This will keep you on the right track, encourage your inner feelings to recall the spirit of the original dream, and allow it to be completed. The following example records an unfinished dream, the experience of reentry, and its final outcome:

> *I was in a place with several rooms joining onto one another, all fairly full of people, talking and laughing in little groups as though they were at a party. I was wondering which group of people to join. But then I went into another room, and there was nobody in there except a "snorter," and I came out again quickly. I have no idea what a "snorter" is, and I didn't actually see it. When I woke up, I felt quite upset, but didn't know why. I was quite depressed for some time afterward.*

During the reentry process the dreamer went back into the room and saw that the mysterious horror in the empty room was just an unpleasant old coat. Then the coat disappeared, and there was a girl she knew and who was cold and crying. She said she felt sorry because this girl was on her own; she cuddled her and felt happy to be with her. Afterward, she explained that the lonely girl in real life suffered from some sort of breathing difficulty like asthma, and was not very sociable. She realized that the old coat represented the image that people tended to see,

and it was unpleasant because those people preferred to avoid contact with it. Further questions and answers were not really necessary. Having been allowed to reach its conclusion, the dream and its message had been accepted and understood. The dreamer was no longer puzzled, and felt very much more understanding and friendly toward the other girl; this encouraged this attitude in other people as well.

Lucid Dreams

Dreams carry an important message far more often than we realize. If there is one message to be learned by heeding our dreams, it is that we have to submit our own will—our outer selves—to that inner message and all it entails. It will be of no value to us if we attempt to control it or dictate to it.

It sometimes happens that, when we are dreaming, our conscious ego intervenes and we become aware that it is "only a dream." Then, if we do not wake up straightaway, we may find that we are able to manipulate the dream characters and direct the dream events. This is known as *lucid dreaming*. Some people recommend it and even look for ways to induce it. It certainly supports the Western principle of acquiring power in your life—the feeling that you should be able to influence events and people and supervise your own subconscious processes.

However, if you help your ego achieve this questionable power, your dream will have lost its originally intended purpose—that of making a point important for your whole psychic development. The student has to listen to the teacher, and the teacher must have authority, otherwise there will no longer be a lesson worth learning. It will simply become an exercise in teacher-control by the student: great fun at the time, but completely useless in the long run. In the following example, the dream became lucid when the dreamer disliked the way events were going:

In the dream I was inside a half-empty industrial building, looking around. It seemed important that I should not be heard or seen. I went up some stairs and into an empty room, which I inspected, thinking in terms of how I could make best use of it. It had a heavy wooden floor, grimy with industry. Then I heard someone moving on the floor above, so I took off my shoes to walk more quietly and tiptoed out of the room down the stairs. I slipped out of the building past the office, trying not to be seen, but someone saw me and came out. I ran away, and they ran after me. The surroundings were unfamiliar, and I didn't know the best direction to run. I hid around the corner of a building behind a pile of empty drums or scrap metal. At this point I realized I was dreaming and decided to alter the dream; almost like a puppet master, I made my pursuer turn around and run the other way. Then I conjured up my own car out of the old drums, made the street look familiar to me, and drove off.

A Trip to Nowhere

You will see that a dream of this sort is not being allowed to arrive at its own rightful conclusion. The dream cycle is being short-circuited at the crucial point. Instead of allowing the inner feelings to select and present a sequence of images, the everyday ego, realizing that it is being "fooled," takes over control. The dream itself from that point will be designed solely to please the ego—the source of power-feeling. Your dream story will have become an ego trip. Your psychic clutch will start to slip, and your vehicle of the self will fail to make progress, though the engine may be racing! This is not how it will

seem to your mind, of course: Your ego and your self-confidence will have received a boost. You are, however, unlikely to meet the unknown part of yourself—merely the comfortable ability to manipulate your own imagination.

The same sort of thing happens involuntarily in a so-called wish-fulfillment dream, in which you dream that your dreams have come true. A condemned man may dream of a reprieve that never actually arrives; a starving person will dream of food; a traveler lost in the desert and dying of thirst will dream of cool streams, or a glass of ice-cold water. Their powerful desires have forced an entry into the closed territory of their subconscious mind, and influenced the outcome of their developing dreams. A wish-fulfillment dream, as a waking memory, can masquerade as a truly predictive dream of the future, but in fact it is an ego trip to nowhere. The following is a typical example:

As a student having just sat my final exams, I was worried about the results, as I knew I could have done much better. I dreamed that the results had come up, and I approached them with dread. One of the lecturers was there, and I said, "Have I failed?" and he said, "Failed? No! You've passed with honors!" The actual results came through a few days later, and in fact I had just barely squeaked by.

Accept the Message

Sharing your dream by relating it to others and listening to their suggestions can help you avoid squandering your dream opportunities. But when a dream becomes lucid, it is up to you alone. When you become aware that you are asleep and dreaming, try to remember that you can use the opportunity for the good. It may well happen that an unpleasant or frightening situation is developing, but try to experience it with patient acceptance: Do not change it for something more pleasant; do not abandon it by waking up. If you do either of these things, the problem will remain unresolved; the solution that is being formulated by your inner feelings will be lost. Remember to remain asleep and continue with your dream, awaiting the outcome with trust and patience. Always allow your dreams to resolve themselves naturally if you can, without interference from the ego, from your own desires. Allow your dream to be the teacher.

The example that follows is of a dream that became lucid, and in which the dreamer persevered under frightening circumstances. It is unusual in that it uses the common but disturbing phenomenon of sleep paralysis to help make a point:

I dreamed that I was asleep in bed and couldn't move. I was trying to get up and out of bed, but was completely paralyzed. I was not alone in the bed, because next to me was a large wolf. I believe that in the dream it was somebody's pet. I felt very scared, first because I could not move, and second because I was aware that wolves are liable to attack people they sense are afraid. This made me all the more scared, because if the wolf started to bite me I couldn't escape. By this time I realized I was sleeping and dreaming that I was trying to wake up. But then I decided to relax and just carry on dreaming, though I was genuinely frightened. The wolf did bite me, as I had feared—on the legs. Then I realized that the bites had allowed the venom that had paralyzed me to run out, and this killed the wolf. After that, I felt perfectly free to move, though I felt rather sorry for the wolf, which was only following its instincts.

The dreamer related this dream to a real and unpleasant situation at work, where a fellow worker was continually harassing her. The moral of the dream seemed to be *Give him enough rope and he'll hang himself*, and she followed the dream's advice. The next day at work the office bully picked on her again, but instead of becoming indignant as she usually did she let him carry on to see what would happen. It was not pleasant, but through the office window she caught sight of the boss arriving. She started to complain loudly and strongly just as the boss walked in. The bully was promptly sacked (and she did feel rather sorry for him); the dreamer had allowed her personal dream message to come to reality in a very helpful way.

Six

DREAMS OF THE FUTURE

And being warned in a dream that they should not return to Herod, they returned to their own country by a different route.

Matthew 2:12

To most people, a dream of the future involves a warning, as in Matthew's version of the biblical Nativity story. Yet simply perceiving something of the future by way of dreams is not a particularly unusual event. Straightforward dreams of what is to be usually relate only to events two or so days ahead.

We could say that the inner self possesses this awareness within itself. It is able to see ahead of the physical body, both in time and space, and in a material, practical sense. The more aware we become of our own inner selves, the closer this awareness of the future comes to our surface minds. In some cases it can even become part of the normal waking awareness. When this happens, we might say that such a person has become psychic.

Warning Dreams

Dreaming of the future is not really an ability, and cannot realistically be considered a neglected function of the brain. Scientific attempts to pinpoint such things experimentally soon become bogged down. Prediction of this sort is not itself predictable, and cannot be stage-managed. Sometimes people set their minds on dreaming about future newspaper headlines, such as national or international events about to happen. I would warn against this kind of practice. Even if these dreamers seem to be successful, they will merely have boosted their own ego and upset the whole purpose of the dreaming process. Real dreams of the future are almost always personal, containing information intended for the dreamer alone.

Dreaming cannot be a predictive art that is carried out intentionally. Becoming aware of the future through dreams cannot be other than involuntary, and the will should not play any part in such dreams. Indeed, they should always be spontaneous. You may, perhaps, wish fervently to know about something in the future. You want to know whether or not such-and-such will happen; whether you will succeed or fail. However, dreams that seem to give this sort of information are always suspect; they may be simply the products of your own wishful thinking. As with the lucid dreams and wish-fulfillment dreams described earlier, your own ego may have forced its attention onto the inner feelings, trying to swing the dream, hoping to influence real-life results. Fervor, anxiety, or intense desire always renders predictive dreams dubious, because they do involve the ego: The quiet voice of wisdom is easily overruled.

A Personal Crisis

Sometimes information given by a predictive dream will have significance only to the dreamer or immediate family circle. In some cases, if the details were told and the people concerned identified, the results could prove embarrassing or hurtful. The following is an example of a domestic dispute foretold by a dream, an interesting mixture of cryptic dream clue and literal fact:

In the dream I was standing at a railway station as a train came in, and passengers were bustling about. Then a voice said: "Look, there's Trevor Huddleston!" I looked, and sure enough there was the tall figure of Bishop Huddleston, just off the train with his baggage. He was carrying an African child cradled in his arms. Then the dream changed, and I was in some rooms. Suddenly a rhino came charging in, knocking my things flying and trampling on everything as I dodged out of the way.

As is well known, the late Father Huddleston was a staunch opponent of racism who served for many years in South Africa and wrote the anti-apartheid book Naught for Your Comfort. *I thought it was rather appropriate in my dream that he was carrying an African child. The following Sunday, I was reading the newspaper when I came across a short paragraph: "Bishop Huddleston has arrived back in England from Africa, to take up his new position as..." I thought, Ha! Look out for the rhino! Almost immediately my partner rushed into the room in a furious temper. She rampaged through my things, hurling my books to the floor and down the stairs, then deliberately trampled on them. I still have no idea what had upset her, but she did apologize later.*

Pharaoh's Dream

This chapter opened with a quote from the New Testament—the brief, matter-of-fact mention of the warning dream of, presumably, all three Wise Men. Probably the best-known example of a warning dream of future events is the Old Testament account of Pharaoh's dream of cows coming up out of the river, predicting devastating drought in Egypt. It was certainly an unusually long-term prediction, relating to fourteen years ahead: seven years of plenty to be followed by seven years of drought. It is a dream that could be decoded quite simply. If such a dream should recur, you don't have to be Joseph (of the many-colored coat) to interpret it. The dream, related in modern language, is as follows:

I was standing in a meadow on the banks of the Nile, and some cows came up out of the river and began to graze. There were seven cows; the number was definite and seemed very important. They were fat, sleek, and healthy looking, and they grazed contently in the meadow. Then seven more cows came up out of the river, but this time they were painfully thin, as though starving to death. Instead of eating the grass they ate up the fat cows, swallowing them whole. And when they had finished eating them, they still looked as thin and starved as before.

Then I woke up; but while I was puzzling about it, I went to sleep again, and this time I dreamed of stalks of wheat. The first stalk had seven ears of wheat, and they were full of fat seeds and healthy. Then another stalk grew up, and this, too, had seven ears of wheat on it, but they were in a very poor condition, thin and withered and quite useless. The poor-quality ears of wheat seemed to eat up the good ones, so that we were left with just the shriveled, useless ears of wheat. Then I woke up again.

The Pharaoh was thought of as the living incarnation of Egypt. So, in effect, his dream was a collective dream for the whole country. Joseph might have thought about that when asked to interpret the dream. The Nile was the great river upon which the whole life of Egypt depended, and its annual floods were essential for the irrigation of crops and grazing land. Joseph might have reasoned that in the Egyptian pantheon Isis was goddess of the Nile, and annual floods were thought to be sent by her. The cow was considered sacred to Isis, and the goddess herself was often depicted as having a horned head. The dream meadow by the river was Egypt's soil, which the Nile could make rich or barren. The condition of the cows coming up from the river represented the quality of the annual flood; each cow represented the good or bad fortune of any particular year.

As though to drive the point home, the ears of wheat in the second part of the dream symbolized the corn harvest suffering the same fate as the rearing of cattle. On its own, perhaps, the idea of an ear of wheat devouring another would seem fairly incomprehensible. But following immediately after the dream of cows, it was made abundantly clear: seven good years, seven bad.

Informative Warnings

Major warning dreams of catastrophic events on a national, or even worldwide, scale originate from a wholly impersonal spiritual source, and perhaps the Pharaoh's dream falls into this category. The world of spirit is not penetrable by human minds, however clever, and such dreams will probably remain a mystery. "Ordinary" dreams of forthcoming disasters, however, stem from the inner feelings of the personal self. Many people relate recurring dreams to a warning about future events, but in my experience convincing dreams of the future seldom occur earlier than two days beforehand. When they do happen, they seldom seem to call for evasive action; they are more likely merely to be informative. The inner consciousness often seems to be aware of future events that may affect us and those close to us. However, it usually seems more concerned with setting right small matters of conscience than with even the approaching death of the dreamer. The following is a rather typical example of a warning dream:

I dreamed that I was on a railway line in thick fog. Ahead of me was what appeared to be a tunnel, or a bridge, which had blood dripping down from it. Soon after this dream, my young niece and I were traveling on the Arlburg express train, after visiting relations in Austria. In the early hours of the morning our train crashed into an unmoving train—the Frankfurt-to-Paris express. I climbed out onto the track after making sure my niece was all right. It was very foggy. There was wreckage, baggage, and blood everywhere. What I had thought was a tunnel or a bridge in the dream was a coach piled on top of another. I learned later that twenty people had been killed, and forty injured.

White-Lie Dreams

Dreams that *do* call for evasive action on the part of the dreamer sometimes seem to use devious means to bring it about. You may experience a vivid warning dream that turns out to be untrue—but has plainly been planned that way for a very good reason. It is a fairly common ploy of the inner feelings to use a "white lie" in order to persuade you to heed the real message. The following is an example of a white-lie dream:

The night before I was due to travel by bus to see my sister, I dreamed I was reading some newspaper headlines: HIGHWAY CARNAGE, *with pictures of vehicles upside down and piled on top of one another. Then it seemed to turn into a TV report, showing injured people being helped away from the road and through some fields.*

I woke with a feeling of panic, and promptly changed my plans for the day, postponing the visit. Later in the day I called my sister's number to make an excuse for not coming, but I had difficulty getting through. It turned out that an hour or two after my bus was scheduled to leave that morning, she'd had a house fire, causing extensive damage to the building and its contents. The firemen and police were in charge when I rang. They said she was unhurt and arranging to stay at a nearby hotel, and they said they would pass my message on to her. She certainly could not have coped with me as a visitor as well as all that hassle! Whether there actually was a highway collision, I don't know. And I'm not sure if the dream was truly a

warning dream or not, but it certainly had the effect of preventing a great deal of unnecessary inconvenience.

It makes sense. Supposing the dreamer had dreamed of the actual event—a fire at her sister's house. She would have called up straightaway in the morning, at which time there would have been no fire—not as yet. The dream would certainly have proved itself when the fire actually occurred, but this is not the point of dreams. As effectively as possible, the dream said, *Don't go!*—and it worked.

Waking Dreams

Waking perceptions of the future can be quite down-to-earth and everyday. They are often almost simultaneous with the event, giving time enough for evasive action, if required. A car driver might "see" an animal cross the highway, preparing him to avoid the real-life animal when it actually appears a few seconds later. Or she might "see" a truck approaching at dangerous speed along a narrow country road—while still out of sight. Experiences like this are not actual dreams, of course, but they are of the same stuff. They are the simple observations of that part of the self that is normally unconscious. Such perceptions may quite frequently be connected with the grim but inevitable prospect of death. Death is a major event, though it seems to hold no fear for the inner consciousness. The example that follows is a true *waking dream*—an incident arranged by the inner self—an encounter between two souls relaying a pictorial message:

I was doing some work in an English church-yard, and stopped to pass the time of day with the verger. He was standing rather awkwardly, straddling a piece of ground that I guessed was probably a vacant grave plot he had to locate.

A churchyard may be a message of a funeral that has yet to happen.

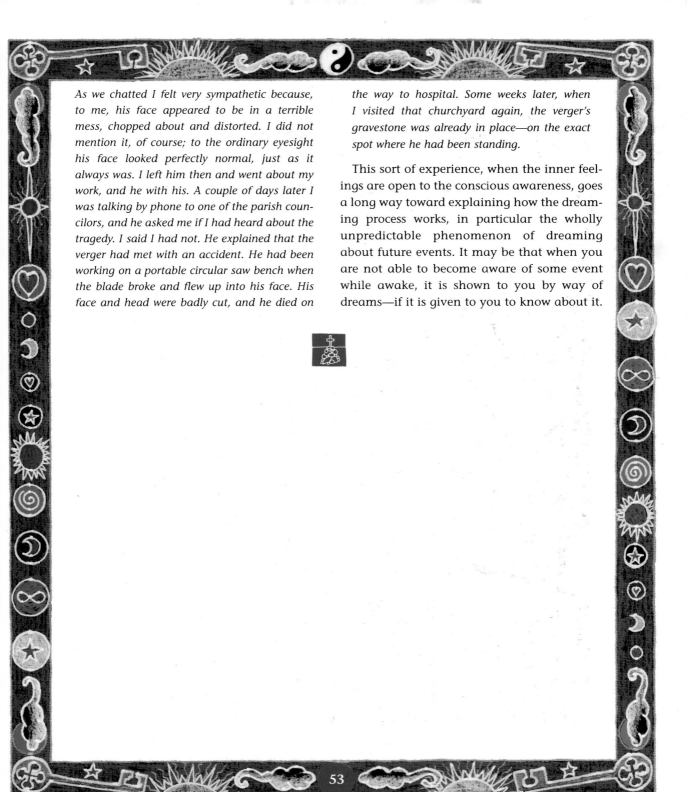

As we chatted I felt very sympathetic because, to me, his face appeared to be in a terrible mess, chopped about and distorted. I did not mention it, of course; to the ordinary eyesight his face looked perfectly normal, just as it always was. I left him then and went about my work, and he with his. A couple of days later I was talking by phone to one of the parish councilors, and he asked me if I had heard about the tragedy. I said I had not. He explained that the verger had met with an accident. He had been working on a portable circular saw bench when the blade broke and flew up into his face. His face and head were badly cut, and he died on the way to hospital. Some weeks later, when I visited that churchyard again, the verger's gravestone was already in place—on the exact spot where he had been standing.

This sort of experience, when the inner feelings are open to the conscious awareness, goes a long way toward explaining how the dreaming process works, in particular the wholly unpredictable phenomenon of dreaming about future events. It may be that when you are not able to become aware of some event while awake, it is shown to you by way of dreams—if it is given to you to know about it.

Seven

DREAMS OF OTHER LIVES

I have spread my dreams under your feet;
Tread softly because you tread on my dreams.

W. B. Yeats, "AEDH WISHES FOR THE CLOTHS OF HEAVEN"

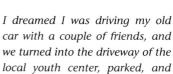

Personal experience may lead you, as it has me, to discover that you may sometimes experience other people's dreams quite unexpectedly—experiencing *their* hopes and fears firsthand, in your own dream.

Intuitive Dreams

It happens quite often when someone you know—possibly someone you care about deeply—chances to occupy your attention in a dream. For example, you may have been thinking about a friend or relative, or he or she may have come to stay with you for a few days. Then, to your surprise, you find you have inadvertently experienced something unique and personal to that individual: an intuitive dream, perhaps a sort of thought-transference dream. The following is an example:

I dreamed I was driving my old car with a couple of friends, and we turned into the driveway of the local youth center, parked, and went inside. While we were there, in came some young men who always cause trouble. They were a gang who always threw their weight around and were quite dangerous. Some people slipped out quietly when they arrived, in order to avoid trouble. My friend was playing (or playing about) on the old piano that was there and hadn't seen them arrive, so I stayed to keep him company, though I really wanted to get out. The gang leader came up to me, and I tried to be casual and polite. He stood deliberately on my toe while I was talking, and it was very painful. I made some feeble joke about him having sharp shoes, or heavy feet, or something like that. Soon afterward, we managed to get out.

It was not until a few days later that I realized this had been a true dream, not about me, but about a boy whom I knew and rather liked. Perhaps I had been thinking about him that night or had feelings for him. I found out that all the events in the dream had actually happened to him. I had not known that the youth center even existed, but a short time later I happened to pass the actual place; the driveway, the signboard, and everything else was exactly as I remembered them in the dream.

This is what is known as a *veridical intuitive dream*—one that includes information that turns out to be true, though you could not possibly have known about it beforehand. For whatever reason, someone else's personal awareness, probably by way of his or her own unconscious sleeping self, has become imprinted upon the blank slate of your own awareness. You will have found out something about this individual that you could not otherwise have known. It has happened to me several times over the years: I arrive at an understanding that does not depend on my own experience, my own memory, or my own power of reasoning.

Dreams of this sort are best not recorded or made public. They would in any case be fairly meaningless without intimate knowledge of the people concerned. They may involve wholly confidential matters that, through the dreaming process, have been divulged to you alone.

The example dream above was about somebody known to the dreamer, but intuitive dreams might happen with regard to someone you *don't* know, someone far away, even someone who may have lived many years before you were born. These dreams, of course, will be no less solid in their base, no less material. Time and space, involving the past, the present, the faraway, or the close at hand, are material concepts that can be bypassed by feelings and dreams.

In the nonmaterial world of dreams, time and space are not barriers to shared experiences. The factors that may have caused you to dream of your friend's experiences are likely to be similarities in the quality of feeling— parallel emotions or empathy, rather than physical closeness. In the friend's intuitive dream, the fact that you are close together physically suggests that thoughts and feelings of sympathy already in your mind have triggered the dream. In a stranger's intuitive dream, a compatible set of thoughts and feelings has, apparently quite by chance, been thrust upon your field of awareness.

Reincarnation Dreams

The Western world is now quite strongly in favor of the idea of reincarnation—of the concept of personal continuation of life after death in another body. We know about the mysterious zone of the collective unconscious that surrounds us all. Yet in a strange way, it seems to be included within our own minds. If all people are linked in this way—and I certainly think we are—it seems reasonable to assume that all worldly experiences are related, too. By remembering our dreams, we know that a traumatic experience in the life of one person can be recalled and reexperienced in the awareness of another. Experience will show that the grief of other people—and grief, it seems, is more likely to be shared than joy— is waiting to be shared, at some deep level of the dreaming state.

A typical reincarnation dream will involve people who are unknown to you. These are obviously real people, not to be confused with the imaginary archetypal characters summoned up by your own subconscious mind. You will seem to be not the old familiar you, but a different you. Invariably, such a dream seems to be focused on the psychological traumas of these complete strangers, perhaps experiencing the events leading up to their death, or to the death of someone else closely involved. Such dreams may be long and substantial, and are always strikingly vivid, often seeming to refer to a particular very definite time and place, or some well-known period of history.

It is not surprising that the dreamers are convinced that they were that person in another life, and they may go to great lengths to verify times and places and incidents, taking them as proof positive of reincarnation. Indeed, there will be little doubt that the original incident, the subject of the dream, actually took place; but it did not happen to the dreamers personally, of course. The identifying feature is extreme emotional trauma—the factor that somehow imprinted a lasting record of a set of experiences, in the form of a solidly real dream, projecting itself as a separate, independent entity. The following example, involving the seventeenth-century period of the English Civil War, is just such a dream:

I seemed to be about seventeen years of age. Four women and I were getting out of a horse-drawn coach. We were all expensively dressed. We were being hurried out of the coach by a man on horseback. He wore a uniform with red tunic and white buckskin breeches. He was very well known to us in the dream, and I remember thinking how strange to see him with such very muddy, dirty breeches: He was usually immaculately dressed. We were outside a small tavern, which was on the corner where two roads met. The horseman said: "I am sorry to disturb you ladies. You will be all right, but we must have the horses." The coach had been drawn by two horses, and another man had already taken them out of the shafts. Riding his own horse, he

cantered away, leading the two coach horses. Inside the inn we all gathered around a large table. An elderly couple (apparently the inn-keeper and his wife) stood at one end of it. After a few moments we heard a tremendous clatter of horses, and we could see a great many men, who looked in through the window. We could see that they were Cromwell's troops of the parliamentary forces. The innkeeper seemed very nervous. He grabbed his gun, which was in the corner near him, and fired blindly. I realized I had been shot. There was some shouted conversation between the inn-keeper and his wife. She was saying something like "Oh, the poor thing!" and he was saying something like "Well what could I do—they'll think we've been harboring them!" That was the end of the dream.

This is not a dream that could be analyzed, because it appeared to carry no personal message for the dreamer; it is simply a record of the dramatic events leading up to a death some three-and-a-half centuries earlier. The dreamer was positive that there had been no trigger events recently in her own life that might have aroused her creative imagination. She had not been reading about the English Civil War, or even thinking about it. This dream involved the apparent death of the dreaming personality; and yet it was the same dreamer, some years later, who experienced this equally vivid dream involving the death of another person:

Another woman and I (I don't think I knew her) and a boy of about twelve were in an empty house, just looking around. We had come up two flights of stairs, and we remarked what lovely big rooms they were. I said to the boy, "There should be a great view of…" (I can't remember where I said), but when we looked through the window it was entirely different from what I had expected, just houses and fields. I walked back to the middle of the room. The boy suddenly opened the sash window and clambered onto the window ledge. I called to him to get down at once, but he just laughed and dangled his legs outside. Obviously he thought it great fun to frighten me and the other woman. He got very excited about something he could see and twisted himself around on the sill. Suddenly he lost his balance and was gone. We both rushed to the window and looked out, and we saw the boy lying in a sort of huddled heap, his legs on the paving and his head and shoulders practically under a hedge. I can't describe the horror and anguish I felt at seeing that small body lying there. I can still see his face, so round, happy, and laughing, and his fair, wavy hair. He would have grown to be a handsome man. I remember he wore a shirt with blue and white checks. I felt guilty at having attracted his attention to the window in the first place.

We tried to analyze the dream, but again it yielded nothing—except the dreamer's own impression of a possible warning not to do or say anything (however well intended) that could lead to disastrous consequences. She felt that had she not mentioned the view, the boy would not have had the idea of climbing out onto the ledge. The warning may well have been apt. Personally, however, I think this was purely another person's dream—a chance to receive, on the communal wavelength, an empathic link across time and space. It contained no message and no psychological significance, apart from itself.

Children's Non-Self Dreams

Access to lost memories of childhood may come flooding back through dreams. Within the family, all kinds of experiences may be shared within the dreaming process, particularly between parent and child, and probably far more commonly than we realize. The waking experience of one member of the family may become the dream of another. You may find yourself dreaming about your child's, your parent's, your brother's, or your sister's experiences. It is not unusual for children to dream about their parents' problems or emotional disturbances, sometimes in realistic terms, seeing events from the parents' point of view, as if through their own eyes; sometimes in the disguise of imagery. The following example was dreamed by a ten-year-old English boy, accurately recalling something his father had experienced when he was the same age, some forty years earlier:

The action in the dream took place in World War I, when three or four soldiers were billeted with us. We were looking through a window into the garden. A very old, sick cat was walking slowly across the green lawn. It had been arranged that one of the soldiers should shoot the cat, to "put it out of its misery," and he had his gun ready. He took aim and shot the cat dead, and I said, "Got him!"

This was confirmed as a perfectly true account when the father happened to mention it some years later. But not all such childhood intuitive dreams involve the family. Children can experience reincarnation dreams, too, as the following example shows, this time a dream so vivid that it was still remembered into adulthood:

I was a Celtic man wearing a rough, hairy garment of some sort of skin, and standing at the edge of the sea on a rocky shore. There was a Roman boat in difficulties some way out, and one of the young men was struggling to reach the shore. I don't think he was wearing the leather body armor that most Roman soldiers wore, though he had a scarlet tunic. Standing in the water, I thrust my spear into his midriff, and as he floundered dying in the waves he looked at me as though to say, Why? Why did you do that? *And I wondered, too. I didn't know why.*

Bridging the Cultural Gap

The dreamer in the last example was in fact of Celtic descent. But sometimes reincarnation dreams will cross racial and cultural boundaries, somehow bridging the gap and combining two distinct sets of ancestral experience. Widely different racial and cultural backgrounds may become merged on the level of the inner feelings, the source of dream expression.

In this dream I was on a lion hunt. I think it was an old rogue lion that had taken to killing cattle, and possibly people, too. We knew it was lying up among some bush-covered rocks at the foot of a rocky hill, and about twelve of us with spears had the spot more or less surrounded. It was very hot. I could feel the sand hot between my toes. The other men were spread out in a semicircle, advancing slowly without making a sound. Their bodies were shining with sweat. I knew them all, friends and neighbors. The rocks were quite vivid, shades of yellow, brown, and gray. I looked back at my companions, all with their spears ready. I was among the rocks, and I realized that I was too far forward from the others, rather isolated and in danger, so I waited for them to draw level. Suddenly I saw the lion. He had a black mane, his rump was

against the rock, and his head was raised in anger. I moved back and made the mistake of turning away for a moment. Then the others all shouted a warning together. I whirled around and tried to raise my spear, but it was too late, the lion was on me. I felt his crushing weight, his mane was smothering me, and I smelled his choking smell. His claws fastened into my back, and his jaws clamped on my neck and the base of my skull.

It was not until long after he was awake and recalling the dream that the dreamer realized that he and all the others in the dream were tribal Africans. Although their faces had seemed so familiar in the dream, they were complete strangers to his waking self. He is an Englishman, and he dreamed the dream in England, though he did spend several years in the African bush, so in some ways could be called an honorary African. The dream would appear to have been a rerun of someone's last moments on earth. The faces of the other hunters were as real to the dreamer, within the dream experience, as those of the members of his family and his friends in waking life. Once again there was no accurate way the dream could be interpreted, personally and specifically, in terms of day-to-day experiences; and yet the dream itself was wholly specific—exact in detail and content.

All Unique and all United

Chapter 5 included the technique of reentering your dream, reexperiencing it, and extending or completing it in order to understand it better. The strange experience of dreaming about other people's lives has encouraged the now well-known technique of hypno-regression, which enables a dreamer apparently to return in time to the substance of a reincarnation dream, to relive it and experience more of it, in greater detail. When

Dreams may incorporate memories of past lives, such as those from the Celtic period.

positive results are obtained, they do much to reinforce the basic belief. However, you might come to the conclusion that there is very little difference between do-it-yourself dream reentry and hypno-regression: If successful, the two produce similar results.

In my view, reincarnation is not something we should try to recapture or hang on to. Our dreams tell us—if we let them—that we have a much higher destiny in store. There is no real difference between a reincarnation dream of death and disaster and an intuitive dream that experiences and shares another's problems. The two are of the same stuff. If there is a difference, it lies in the understanding of them, in the passions and perceptions of the dreamer. The sharing of trauma at this deep level is a personal and not a secondhand experience. In the dream itself, there is no difference between reincarnation and not-reincarnation. All are unique, yet all are united.

THE SYMBOLISM OF DREAMS

To dream you cut off the head of a green goose
Signifies joy and recreation.

Thomas Tryon, A TREATISE ON DREAMS

*S*ome of the explanations given in old dream books—like Thomas Tryon's seventeenth-century work—are fairly unfathomable. Then again, the unconscious mind *is* unfathomable. We know that the personal unconscious receives all the thoughts and impressions that have occupied our attention during waking hours, and quite probably things that may have escaped our attention, too. Anything our waking mind has found troublesome is, in effect, mulled over subconsciously, clothed in a fresh guise, and re-presented to our conscious mind in a form that we may find more acceptable.

Even if we fail to understand the symbolism, it is best to accept our dream with an open mind. It would be wonderful if we were able to understand everything we need to know to cope with anything that may happen. Until then, though, the dreaming process initiated by the unconscious mind is working toward a whole and wholly human state—one in which nothing really need influence the psyche unfavorably.

Everything that happens in a dream is a symbol of something. Those symbols that feature in personal dreams, on a personal level, will be your own personal symbols. However, these very same symbols may hold a totally different meaning for someone else. For example, to dream of a black cat may be a symbol of good luck to you; to someone else it may equally well be a symbol of bad luck. Or it may be a symbol to one person of warmth and friendliness, while to another it may symbolize uncaring aloofness.

Nevertheless, when symbols occur in dreams that have emerged into your awareness from the collective unconscious—the great dreaming store that is common to all humankind—the symbols, although they may represent something personal to you, may be shared to some extent. Nobody can really fathom the depths of this great ocean of shared experience. It is something that

Is dreaming of a black cat a symbol of good or bad luck?

has been building up since our ancestors first evolved.

Some of the shared symbols of our dreams may have originated even before that long, drawn-out process was complete, and may also feature in the awareness of animals—symbols that relate to the basics of a lifestyle familiar to our ancient forebears—with sunrise, sunset, moonlight; the search for food; and the threat of capture by enemies being strong components. These symbols are some of the most frequently occurring in dreams. Of course, they may be modified or disguised. So let us consider some of the dream symbols most frequently encountered.

Abbey

If you are of European origin, the abbey that comes to your awareness will most probably be a ruin—impressive and beautiful, but long ago reduced to a roofless shell. (In Britain most such ruins are due to the activities of King Henry VIII during the Reformation early in the sixteenth century.) There are several associations of ideas that may have triggered your dream. First there is the idea of an ancient, self-contained community, with power and authority over the people, whose money and property were liable to disappear into the abbey's tithe barn or the abbot's counting house. Then there is the idea of ancient splendor destroyed to make way for new ideas, or a feeling of being drawn back by outmoded ways of thinking.

Alternatively, there is the idea of powerful religious feelings, possibly long gone and half forgotten, or memories of devotion and prayer no longer practiced. Or the abbey can symbolize a parent or parent figure on whom you used to rely. Much depends on your own feelings during and immediately after the dream: Was there a feeling of reverence, or of panic, or of beauty, or of regret? These are important pointers to the nature of your dream and will relate to your past, present, and hopes for the future.

See also **ALTAR, CHURCH, RUINS**

Abuse

In your dream, if someone is hurling abuse or insults at you, or if you are shouting abuse at someone else, there is usually a hidden element of self-criticism. Sometimes when you are feeling guilty, your dream implies that other people are blaming you for something similar that you know does not deserve abuse. This may be your own subconscious way of covering up your true feelings by a little pretense—a dream charade that makes you feel better. In effect your dreaming self will have changed the subject for your own waking peace of mind.

See also **ACCUSATIONS**

Abyss

This primeval pit can take many forms. Dreams of great heights, great depths, and the sensation of falling are closely allied. The abyss can appear disguised as a coal mine, quarry, hole in the road or backyard, deep pond, whirlpool, the edge of a cliff—anything that has a similar shape or similar capacity to swallow up anyone unfortunate enough to drop inside.

For some religious people, it can represent the most basic of world images—the Creation, the fall from grace, the very fact of living on a material earth rather than sharing the world of immateriality with the angels. In these broad terms it can imply excessive concern with material interests and a warning that the dreamer has been ignoring higher principles in favor of unreasonable financial gain, or overvaluing social status.

The symbol of the abyss represents the personal unconscious. It may be a general reminder of the constant cycling that takes place continuously within the psyche. An abyss dream can warn against negative thinking, against neglecting matters that are your responsibility. It could be a stern warning against pushing personal problems onto others when you should be dealing with them yourself during waking hours.

On a still more practical level, the abyss can represent fear of loss and a sense of danger—fear of losing your position at work or in society, for instance, or of losing your way professionally; something you find worrying yet difficult to pinpoint. It can warn against giving way to immoral impulses. It can also symbolize femininity; and for a man, it can highlight fears of sexual inadequacy. To dream of an abysslike situation demands urgent attention to the circumstances of your daily life: a warning best not ignored.

See also BASEMENT, CAVE, DUNGEON, PIT

Accident

Nowadays most dreams of accidents involve driving or finding your car damaged. To dream that you actually crash into another car—or seem to have been in grave danger of doing so—involves the use of symbols at a very basic level. Cars, travel, metal objects in general, are all symbols of materiality. When they are functioning well, they represent your own normal progress through life. But when accidents happen or there is a risk of an accident, the implication is that either you or those close to you are in danger of material loss or are coming up against financial or legal problems.

To dream that someone else has damaged your car implies that another person is the one in trouble, but it involves a material situation you put yourself into or have built up. For instance, suppose you have retired and your son or daughter has taken over your business. To dream of finding your car smashed, or even totaled, suggests that you believe your child is mishandling the business you worked so hard to establish. To dream that you are driving when an accident or near-accident with another vehicle occurs or is imminent—perhaps involving a train at an open rail crossing (a common dream situation)—suggests that you are running up against unavoidable difficulties. The key factor, then, is that your journey through life is being impeded by material difficulties.

See also CAR, DRIVING, ROAD

Accusations

There is usually an element of personal guilt hidden somewhere inside a dream in which someone is making an allegation against you—or when you are accusing them. If the dream is of a real-life situation, of course you will recognize it; if not, you may take it as a hint to "consider the beam in thine own eye"—it may turn out to be yourself who deserves the criticism!

See also ABUSE

Acne

Your complexion or the condition of your skin often symbolizes your habitual way of expressing your persona—the element of yourself that you want others to see. If the dream is of pimples or marks on your face, the implication is that your faults are on the surface, obvious to others. If the spots are on a part of the body normally kept covered up, the implication is that you are keeping some unsavory truth about yourself a secret from others (a common enough situation!) and feeling worried lest it be discovered.

See also CLOTHES, NAKED

Acorn

Tall oaks from little acorns grow originally referred to a school student excusing his imperfections. This fruit of the impressive oak tree is an apt symbol of the small beginnings from which great things may arise. Like other nuts, the acorn can also symbolize hidden properties of the mind. (Refer to the final example dream in Chapter 4.)

See also EGGS

Acrobatics

Saying that people "bend over backward" to achieve their aims means that they go to great lengths to make or hide a point, fulfill a task, or accommodate someone else's needs. When someone you know seems to have become an acrobat, it may be that either you or they have made the best of a situation or have performed a metaphorical somersault to find a more secure foothold in life—a better job, perhaps, or a more rewarding position in society.

See also AGILITY

Acting

A dream involving anonymous actors performing may imply that other people you are associated with are unreliable or insincere. If you are the one doing the acting, it is likely that you are the one who is not being altogether honest. Yet it is common in dreams that the actors you see are recognizable characters from TV or some other medium. In this case their presence in your dream underscores the feeling you have for them. If, for instance, you feel that a certain soap opera is typical of everyday life, and if your dream features characters from that series, the actors are setting the scene for you as a normal, everyday situation. But if you feel the show represents a spiteful or deceitful attitude, say, then that kind of behavior will be the context of your dream. Always remember your own feelings with regard to these dream figures: They will provide the clue.

See also THEATER

Adversary

This mysterious, threatening character is one of the archetypes of the collective unconscious, and can sometimes be identified as the personal shadow itself. The symbol represents any major factor that you have not been accepting in waking life and have allowed to build up in your subconscious mind until it has assumed menacing proportions. Any specific worry or temporary difficulty not already dealt with by your conscious mind may appear in dreams—but as an assailant rather than an adversary, and the situation tends to be ongoing. Try to face up to the image and identify it. Though menacing, it cannot really harm you. It is already a part of you.

If you are a religious person, an image of the Devil as an adversary may represent everything within your own character that you consider belongs to his department: everything that is undesirable. An aggressive or threatening figure, person, or animal may carry some kind of identifying feature so that you will be able to relate it to your work, recreation, or family life. If you can isolate and name the fear, you will be better able to handle it.

See also ASSAILANT, DEMON, OPPONENT, XENOPHOBIA

A dream involving actors may indicate that certain people are being less than honest.

Advice

If you dream you are being given advice by a reliable person—someone known to you personally—you will probably be able to relate this to an incident in real life and understand what the dream is trying to tell you. However, you may be advised by a wise person unknown to you in real life. If so, it may be a part of your own self—an archetype of the collective unconscious. You would do well to heed this person's advice; it might be of great value. If you are the one giving advice to someone else, this could be a warning that you are interfering. Look at all these possibilities objectively and thoroughly.

See also **GODDESS, KING, QUEEN, WISE PERSON**

Agility

You or another may perform amazing physical feats or contortions in your dreams. The inner feelings that supply your dream images are not bound by physical laws: In dreams, unencumbered by your sleeping body, you can defy the force of gravity! The dream may be pointing out that you have been evading your responsibilities or are hiding some truth that would be better released. Make sure you are not hurting someone's feelings in real life; this can do more harm than you might think.

See also **ACROBATICS**

Alarm

This could take the form of a wake-up call, a sudden disturbance, or a descent into panic. Present-day terrorist attacks have triggered a massive increase in the frequency of dreams that are in some way based on the principle of alarm. General fears are understandable, but they should not be allowed to cloak the more personal meaning: the call for personal action, in whatever sphere.

See also **ASSAILANT, BATTLE, ROOSTER**

Alligator

When they feature in your dream, creatures of this type—alligators or crocodiles, komodo dragons, giant lizards, dinosaurs—usually represent a set of emotions you probably thought were extinct but that have merely lain dormant for a long time. You may perhaps look over a familiar wall in your dream and discover a swamp full of frightening creatures on the other side. You would probably stir these monsters to fury if you poked them with a stick or risked venturing into their territory. They represent dark desires you thought were long gone but that still remain within your own unconscious mind—part of the shadow that could reemerge at any time. When people do something out of character and say, "I don't know what got into me!" most likely it was one of their own dream crocodiles or alligators making its presence known.

See also **CROCODILE, DRAGON, MONSTER**

Altar

An altar can be seen as the heart of worship within your feelings, and the place that you would not want to see defiled with anything you normally dissociate from that feeling of devotion. Different people are devoted to different things. At the heart of your feelings, symbolically, is the Table of the Altar, the *Sanctum Sanctorum*. It may be associated with the feelings you have toward another person and is very often connected with a sexual relationship. Perhaps you feel that your relationship is not generally acceptable for one reason or another, and you would like to make it so. If you remember placing some-

Dreaming of an angel suggests reassurance, support, and guidance.

thing on the altar in your dream, take careful note of it, and think around it. Remember also if anything was already on the altar. To summarize, the symbol represents either a principle that you already consider to be beyond reproach or a circumstance that you would dearly like to make respectable, free from guilt.

See also **ABBEY, CHURCH**

Ambulance

A dream ambulance would seem a fairly straightforward symbol of action being taken to put right something that is considered wrong or that the dreamer has been suspecting or worrying about. It may even feature in a realistic, predictive dream of an accident or of medical problems that may arise. Predictions of this nature may be referring to the dreamer or to a family member, but the symbol may have a more subtle meaning. The illness or injury may be no more than a wrong opinion—a mistaken accusation, perhaps; the ambulance symbolizes that this misunderstanding is about to be cleared up or put right. It features quite often, too, when dreamers have been worrying about their sexual orientation or similar matters not usually thought of as illnesses.

See also **HOSPITAL**

Anchor

"Will your anchor hold in the sea of life..." This well-known hymn points out the usual religious significance of an anchor. But it can also mean something more in the nature of a millstone—something to weigh you down and hold you back. You will need to decide which of these meanings is the appropriate one: something to depend on, or something to escape from.

See also **BAGGAGE, MUD, OBSTACLES**

Angel

Precisely what an angel means for you will depend almost entirely on your own experience of life—your own ideas of what constitutes an angel and what you suppose the function of an angel to be. In most religion-based cultures, angels are perceived as divine messengers made of light. Taken from the collective unconscious, they are able to represent whatever the will of God is perceived to be by the individual. Nowadays, perceptions of the will of God can vary to a frightening degree. What does an angel mean to you personally? In the West it is usual to think of angels as creatures who can be relied on to give a helping hand when it is most needed. They are gentle beings filled with love, who are forgiving, sexless, and nonjudgmental.

However, in some Eastern cultures, angels are thought of as divine administrators doling out judgment, punishment, or reward, as deserved. They may be depicted as fierce, masculine creatures wielding a sword or ax. In this case, an angel may bear a message that you do not want to listen to in waking life. If an angel appears in typical Western form as a winged, robed, perhaps golden-haired being filled with love, then the message it carries will be one of reassurance, condolence, possibly gentle reproof. Mystics say that angels can assume whatever form and appearance they wish. Should a *real* angel appear before you in your dawn dream, the message will be for you alone.

See also **JUDGE**

Animals

Dreams in which the dreamer seems actually to be an animal may be reflections of the world dream (Chapter 3). Such dreams may even hint at reincarnation, or dreaming another's dream (as described in Chapter 7). Somebody to whom animals are particularly familiar—a farmer, for instance—may find that they are included in a dream merely to set the scene in familiar surroundings. However, where this is obviously not the case, and animals have featured strongly in a personal dream, personal interpretation will be needed. Heavy, horned animals carry with them the idea of powerful masculinity best not disturbed, and as a simple warning may suggest that you should take care in your daily life not to upset the kind of man who might fit this category.

A wild forest animal, such as a startled deer among the trees, may be telling you that you have been evading social obligations, taking refuge instead in the forest of the mind.

A dream of your pets may simply be offering you a message regarding them. But many amazing examples of animal dreams have been recorded when the dreamer is working well on his or her dream life. The personal shadow itself can take the form of a fierce animal, often a travesty or distortion of a domestic pet known to you. It is a frightening apparition, but a fairly common device, and one that draws attention to the fact that this demonic creature in the dream represents something that is actually very close and familiar. It is a part of your own subconscious that has built itself up into this frightening form, and requires your understanding.

See also **BIRDS, BULL, COW, EAGLE, ELEPHANT, HORSE, PARROT, PIG, ROOSTER, WOLF, ZOO**

Antique

In dreams an antique is usually a symbol for something or some relationship you feel to be very precious and permanent, but which you do not feel able to express in more realistic terms. If it is a container of some sort—a chest, a closet, or a casket—you will probably feel that it contains something of great value. Purely on a psychological level, it can probably be decoded as a symbol involving your own sexual impulses or a hoped-for sexual relationship. But in mystical terms, while not precluding the sexual element, it is likely to imply that you are being offered the chance to pursue a spiritual path. It is very much a personal dream object, and only you, the dreamer, can decode it thoroughly enough to extract its complete meaning. Something very important is certainly involved, and it is up to you to decide what it is and what actions are needed.

See also **ARCHAEOLOGY**

Archaeology

The symbol is focused on digging up secrets from the past. If something is revealed, or seems about to be revealed from its hiding place in the earth, it is probably something coming to awareness from the depths of your own unconscious mind. The implication is that it has been there for a very long time; it may even be something inherited from your ancestors—some fact that has been kept secret from you but should now be revealed. It will certainly be significant for your life, and may be something of great value. Only you can find out what it really means.

See also **ANTIQUE**

Art / Artist

It may be that artwork is something familiar to you and typical of your everyday experiences, in which case it merely sets the scene for your dream. But if art does not normally occupy your attention, some sort of creative work is clearly being carried out or planned: Something is depicted as being put on display for the world to see. The inspiration for your artwork is likely to arise from your own personality and represents an aspect of yourself that you feel shows you in a good light. The artist could be one of the archetypes of the collective unconscious, the persona perhaps, painting a prettied-up view of your own character. Take care that you are not falsifying your situation in some way.

See also **PAINTING, STITCHCRAFT**

Assailant

Broadly similar to the archetype of the adversary, the assailant represents matters that you have found challenging or disturbing, but have not been able to deal with during waking hours. Such things are invariably pushed into the inner feelings, where they are liable to become absorbed by the shadow. A dream assailant tends to represent something from outside yourself. A dream adversary tends to represent a permanent condition existing within the self. The actual nature or identity of your dream assailant tends to remain unknown, and it may be felt simply as an unseen, brooding presence. If you are able to reenter your dream (see Chapter 5), you may be able to identify it, and the dream itself may offer a solution. Even if you cannot do this, it may yield to your personal interpretation if you think around every aspect of the dream, noting your emotions at every stage and listing any associated themes that you find even vaguely upsetting.

See also **ADVERSARY, OPPONENT, XENOPHOBIA**

Baby

You may, of course, dream about your own or somebody else's baby in a straightforward way, without any need for decoding. However, the innocent child-self is a major archetype of the collective unconscious—yourself, in fact, looking innocently at the world around you. The symbol of a very young baby is more likely to refer to some particular aspect of the self, to some unfamiliar inner dimension that has recently been "born" or come to realization. Otherwise, a baby may represent any new life, new venture, new psychological direction, new career, new way of looking at yourself—anything, in fact, that seems newly to have come to life.

See also **CHILD**

Baggage

From the point of view of your inner feelings, the part of you able to select dream images, all life is a journey, and everything that you carry with you—especially your passions and desires, loves and hates, hopes and fears, likes and dislikes—constitutes your baggage. Some people carry so many bags that life becomes a burden to them. If your dream is telling you that your own burden has become too great, take time out to quiet your thoughts and feelings. The only passions that are really important for you at such a time are the quiet passions of faith, patience, and sincerity. The more often you can find time to quiet your thoughts in this way, the lighter your life's baggage is likely to be.

See also **OBSTACLES**

Ball

Chapter 1 included the idea that the nonmaterial self is in some ways like a ball; the more a person progresses toward wholeness, the more spherical the self will seem. But a ball, of course, is a common plaything for a child or a household pet, and its image can carry a hint of the carefree but not particularly helpful pursuits of others. This in turn can imply that the dreamer has felt left out of things or isolated, physically or emotionally.

Football, soccer, baseball, or other major games are so widely popular that they can carry dream significance with regard to relationships. A professional game can represent not recreation, strife, or competition so much as the majority viewpoint. Everyone attending a match seems to be slanted in one specific direction, supporting his or her side. Songs and chants strengthen the feeling of "all for one and one for all." The ball sometimes seems to be the only odd one out. Dreams involving these things, therefore, can carry a powerful feeling that the dreamer is either firmly in or firmly out of step with the most widely held popular view, and is therefore in danger of ignoring the needs of some individual or minority group—or conversely of courting unpopularity by swimming against the tide of opinion.

See also **BALLOON, PLAYING**

Ballet

Whether you are taking part or merely watching the dancers, this kind of theatrical performance in your dream is sure to have a very personal significance. Display, poise, and confidence are at its root, and the dream may be telling you that you are selling yourself short in these respects. Ballet involves a type of stylized romance, like an old-fashioned ceremony of courtship, perhaps, with all the participants following the rules expected of them. The dancers, in effect, are demonstrating how something should be done and are admired for their skill. The symbolism needs to be thought about very carefully. It may involve admiration or a hint of envy.

See also **DANCE, THEATER**

Balloon

Balloons are typically round, light, and airy, sometimes floating freely in the air. Children's playthings, they are often brightly colored and are associated with parties; they burst easily. Dream balloons have two basic appearances. The spiritual balloon, like a bubble or a sphere floating in space, is a symbol of inner feelings, which are unaffected by the earthly problems. The materialistic balloon is both an ephemeral symbol of hedonistic enjoyment on the one hand and childlike innocence on the other. The materialistic balloon of pleasure or innocence is liable to burst without warning and bring the carefree mood it represents to an abrupt end. Only you, the dreamer, can decide which category fits your personal balloons and interpret the dream accordingly.

See also **BALL**

Ballot

Voting is all about exercising free choice. You have at least two alternatives, and now is the time to select one, for better or worse. You may well have reached a crossroads in your life—practical, moral, or spiritual—and unless the dream itself points out the best choice, the dream is probably a reflection of your indecision.

See also **CROSSROADS**

Bamboo

Bamboo is a universal symbol of flexibility, the principle of yielding to a more powerful force, allowing unpleasantness to flow over you in a way that will not be of long-term damage. A stout tree may be snapped off or uprooted in a gale, but the slender bamboo merely bows its head and allows the disturbance to pass safely over. It can represent an eminently mature act of humanity, to allow somebody to rage like a hurricane without retaliating, without making a hurtful comment or clever put-down that may only make matters worse. The bamboo is a reminder to let it go rather than fight against unreasonable behavior on the part of others. Then, of course, the shoe may be on the other foot: You may be the one forcing others. They may respond in a bamboolike manner while *you* rage and shout. In either case, take your dream as a hint and allow the storm or unpleasantness to pass safely.

See also **AGILITY**

Barn

Dream buildings frequently symbolize your own self. Whatever the building contains—or what you in the dream think it might contain—represents yourself, including your hopes and fears, and in particular perhaps feelings of guilt or a sense of not being good enough. A barn is a storehouse where useful things should be kept. If the storage space is bare, perhaps you feel your own life is empty or has little worth. If so, your dream is telling you that this is an illusion: We are all full of worth. Perhaps in the dream you are aware of a mysterious presence in the barn, something unseen or unidentifiable: This is likely to be your own shadow, characteristics you do not wish others to know about, that

you do not even want to acknowledge as your own. The shadow may represent a problem you have pushed aside and do not want to face up to. But this is *your* barn, so if you explore it thoroughly you will come away richer for the experience.

See also **SHACK, STORE, VASE**

Basement

An underground room beneath a building is a fairly common theme in psychologically oriented personal dreams, and a powerful symbol of your own personal unconscious, the dark container of the yin into which all your waking thoughts find their way—including everything that your conscious mind has rejected. In this dream basement you may be supporting a menacing unknown presence—your own shadow, composed of all the personal characteristics that you would rather not expose to view.

Write down all the details as soon as you awaken; try to remember everything about that dream basement, everything you saw or sensed while you were there. All these hidden images need to be drawn out and examined: They are all part of your own psyche that needs exploring.

See also **ABYSS, DUNGEON, PIT**

Battle / Battlements

Attack or defense in your dream tends to reflect your personal situation in real life. You may feel that everyone is against you, or perhaps you feel locked out of where you want to be, unable to succeed in a tricky situation. It is a common experience to feel under siege, the odd one out, or fear that your position is being endangered by the actions of others. Life often feels like a battlefield when you try to improve your material situation; dreams of this nature call for a re-examination of your lifestyle. It could be warning you against selfish behavior. Could your attitude be improved? Think not only of your own immediate needs; as you contemplate your long-term goals also bear in mind the importance of your relationships with others.

See also **FORTRESS**

Birds

Some people are frightened of birds; others love them and would like to spend most of their time thinking about them and watching them. Birds are said to be direct descendants of dinosaurs, so they express the idea of a primeval life force. As members of the animal kingdom, birds tend to be competitive and parochial: They look after their own, putting family and group before the general welfare. Bird nature may be cold and selfish, but they are programmed to warn others by their cries when danger is about.

A host of meanings have traditionally been associated with birds: the bluebird of happiness, the white dove of peace, the black raven of fate, the stork of childbirth, the owl of wisdom, the vulture of death, the freedom of the wild goose, the mindless repetition of the parrot, the thieving of the magpie. And then there is the peacefully beautiful, as represented by the hummingbird, the sunbird, or the kingfisher.

A flock of birds can suggest migration, seeking refuge in a faraway place or arriving from a distance. It might equally symbolize wasted efforts or natural disaster. Many peasant farmers have watched helplessly as flocks of birds devoured their crops.

Dead birds are a common dream expression of lost freedom. In many cultures birds symbolize the human soul: Following the death of someone known to the dreamer, a large white bird such as a swan is seen flying away. This typically symbolizes the soul leaving the body.

See also **ANIMALS, EAGLE, PARROT, ROOSTER**

Blood

For the physical body, blood is the essence of life; dreaming about blood thus has to carry an earthbound or materialistic message. Occasionally whole nations seem fairly obsessed with the image of blood, their people seeing themselves as noble, longsuffering, and prepared for sacrifice, so the meaning of blood as a dream symbol will depend on your own cultural background. In dreams that reflect the world dream, blood carries implications of aggression and selfish conflict. In the great majority of dreams of blood or bloodstained clothing, however, the implication is physical trauma or concern over illness, possibly involving the heart or circulatory system.

See also **DOCTOR**

Boat

A vessel sailing peacefully symbolizes safe passage over the depths of emotion, undisturbed by the more turbulent aspects of sexual attraction. The image of a stormy sea is closely connected with the boat symbol, and a storm almost invariably refers to stormy emotional scenes and wildly erratic relationships. As with any symbol of transport, it includes the basic idea of a journey—either in general terms, through life, or more specifically from one place to another. Large ocean liners may carry the simple practical message of overseas travel.

For individuals who are connected with boats in their daily lives, the symbol may merely be setting the scene for your dream, placing it on a workday basis.

See also **JOURNEY, SEA, WATER**

Books

Unless they are plainly antique and valuable in themselves, dream books tend to represent their own contents—and the idea of knowledge and information kept in store ready for use when required. They can symbolize virtue, wisdom, the knowledge of a learned person, or an academic institution of some sort. In spiritual dreams an open book may reveal some information necessary for the dreamer's spiritual progress, in words or pictures. However, in any dream there is usually the extra dimension of personal familiarity—what do books mean to the dreamer? To some, books suggest education that is unavailable, something only the privileged few have access to. To others, books carry a more positive meaning: satisfaction, romance, reliability, and sufficiency. A book is usually more than a simple scene-setter in a dream; it is a symbol that can be thought about, and interpreted according to the dreamer's personal experience and needs.

See also **LIBRARY**

Bread

Bread is "the staff of life," age-old symbol of the means of livelihood and the meeting of basic needs. Depending on the dreamer's own culture and background, bread can signify money, the means of living; it can imply on the one hand plenty, or on the other hand poverty ("on the breadline"). To dream that you have run out of bread to eat implies that your usual way of earning a living has disappeared or that your resources are being used up. You may be harboring worries over your future security and income.

See also **FEAST, FOOD**

Bridge

This is a potent symbol: A bridge always represents the means to cross over or surmount some obstacle. A bridge over water calls for a personal interpretation of the symbol of water, considering its clarity or muddiness, its depth or shallowness, its sexual or emotional implications in your waking life. It may refer to some emotional or sexual issue that you would rather not face directly. The bridge may suggest a way to overcome this problem. Dark or muddy water implies guilt connected with your own flow of feelings; clean water shows that feelings of guilt are not involved, but you still do not wish to become involved.

Looking down from a bridge puts stress on whatever is or flows beneath and represents a convenient way of observing or appraising whatever may be at the root of a problem: possibly something you feel aloof about or do not want to have direct contact with. You might be looking down a busy highway, implying that you do not wish to follow the crowd; a quiet and lonely lane may imply the opposite—if you have been feeling isolated, you may be seeking to rejoin society and become involved.

Looking up at a bridge from below carries the opposite meaning: You, the dreamer, will be wondering how you can surmount your problems, wondering if you can climb up from the difficulties of your waking life.

A bridge over another road or a railroad can imply arrogance—a feeling of superiority—or a sense of longing to join in other people's activities. A bridge could feature in the dream of a "fugitive," someone who feels isolated and is looking for a way to rejoin the world at a more fulfilling level.

See also **FORD, JOURNEY, PATH, WATER**

A bridge is a powerful symbol showing how to overcome an obstruction or problem.

Broom

Bear in mind the old adage *A new broom sweeps clean*, and see if this fits your current lifestyle or prospects. It could mean either that a cleanup is needed or is imminent (and this cleanup may be physical, material, moral, cultural, or spiritual), or that a drastic reorganization that will affect you is taking or is about to take place, but it should be all to the good.

See also **DIRT, DUST, WEEDING**

Bugs

To dream of insects and bugs can mean different things, depending upon your individual attitude toward such life forms. The most common implication is that unwanted intruders are adversely affecting your life. Ask yourself: *What does this symbol mean to me personally? And what were my feelings during the dream and immediately afterward?* Try to relate these feelings to recent real-life situations, and take careful stock of your life. It may be that a health or hygiene problem needs urgent attention.

See also **ADVERSARY, ASSAILANT**

Bull

The bull is a powerful animal that is usually seemingly docile, but potentially violent and dangerous. On the level of the world dream, a bull epitomizes animal-based clannishness and difficult social access. A wholly male symbol, the dream bull often represents an actual person with overly masculine characteristics; a person who in normal times will live and let live, but who may prove a dangerous enemy if his interests are challenged or if nonbullish ideas are introduced into his domain. As usual, interpretation depends on the dreamer's own life experiences. For example, a farmer may have a special familiarity with bulls; a bullfighter certainly will. Their imagery may be quite different from most.

See also **ANIMALS, COW**

Bully

A bullying character in your dream can often be related to a real-life situation. If you really have bullying problems, search the dream carefully to see if it offers a solution. Conversely, it may be that you personally are doing the bullying, in which case the dream should be taken as a timely warning against unacceptable behavior. A bullying dream may be telling you that you have been acting unfairly; to dream you are hitting someone usually means that you are causing him or her undeserved grief. Think about it carefully and seek a solution.

See also **ADVERSARY, ASSAILANT, OPPONENT, WOLF**

Bulrushes

Stream- or pondside vegetation often carries an air of mystery about it. Moses and various mythological characters were supposed to have been found abandoned in the rushes and rescued as babies, later to achieve greatness. Reeds and rushes afford shelter from danger, a metaphorical shelter from the emotions symbolized by the water, or the exposure symbolized by sun and weather. Bulrushes therefore, are a hiding place for something that may be either good or bad, something likely to emerge and make itself known.

See also **WATER**

Burglar

A common dream symbol is an intruder gaining access into someplace he or she has no right to be. A dream involving burglars may represent fears about security or it may have a more deeply hidden meaning: meddling in someone's affairs, perhaps, trying to uncover secrets, and seeking an unfair advantage. A burglary dream needs careful decoding by taking into account all the characters and situations involved.

See also **ASSAILANT, ENEMY**

Burial

The most likely meaning of a dream burial, especially when a ceremony is involved, is that a way of life or set of circumstances has come to an end and new beginnings are to be expected. Depending on the scale of the burial in the dream, a simple affair may imply that something is being hidden from view; something that ought to be made public, perhaps, is being kept secret. It could be that your own problems are being pushed out of sight when you should be dealing with them as they arise.

See also **DEATH, FUNERAL**

Cactus

Any thorny or prickly plant in a dream carries the implication of difficulties or dangers that must be faced in real life. They also suggest an underlying connection with the world dream, because plants sometimes represent aggression and selfish behavior. Pioneer psychiatrist Alfred Adler (see Chapter 4) formulated the theory of the inferiority complex triggered by the will to power—which, he believed, underlay much human unpleasantness. Cacti and cactuslike plants grow in desert conditions, so this dream image may be telling you to look for a practical way out of your problems and to have more confidence both in yourself and in others.

See also **THORNS**

Calendar

Like the clock, a calendar symbolizes the passage of time, often expressing urgency and the need for action. It can be a reminder that time is limited and there are things to do. It may simply be reminding you of an important date or a forgotten anniversary. It may symbolize the possibility of a change from the merely mundane level of dream experience, offering a hint of real spiritual contact.

Of course, a calendar can refer backward as well as forward: It may draw your attention to some forgotten event that has significance in your life today. When other dream images are involved as well, they should be interpreted with dates and times in mind.

See also **CLOCK**

Canal

A canal differs from a river chiefly in that it is man-made. Water as a dream symbol represents the emotions or the sex drive. A mighty river implies the flow of these powerful emotions and feelings over which you have no control. Canals are much more personal, for they represent your own emotional route through life: the direction of your sexual desires as they have been conditioned by your own experiences. The water will probably be muddy, without the impersonal current of life to keep it clear. The dream may be advising you to clean up your act in real life.

See also **RIVER, WATER**

Candle

Religions often make use of symbols. Although candles, as a rule, play no part in the story of a religion or the history of its religious practices and beliefs, many religions employ candle imagery. This imagery is chiefly for sentimental reasons. Believers who consider themselves to have direct contact with the Divine Will seldom feel the need to make use of candle imagery. On the face of it, a candle is something of a phallic symbol, implying fertility and rebirth. A religious dimension adds the fire of spirit: divine light that will point the way.

In the West candles are a favorite theme of Christmas cards. In some cultures candles in containers are set to float on water—itself a symbol of emotional and sexual depths. Such customs go a long way toward explaining the candle as a dream symbol.

See also **ALTAR, CARVINGS, STATUE**

Car

If you normally use a motorized vehicle in your day-to-day life, so that it is almost second nature to drive wherever you need to go, the dream symbol of a car represents merely your own "vehicle" through life, your own progress. For people who never drive and who need to walk everywhere, the corresponding symbol might be a footpath, a track, a pair of shoes, or merely the physical sensation of walking. The car makes a useful symbol in this respect, because whatever happens to you along the road of life can be represented by a dream incident affecting your car—it might get scratched or smashed up or run out of gas; you might be carrying passengers, and other drivers might behave in various ways—all these things relate to your own personal fortunes or misfortunes. If your car breaks down in the dream, your inner feelings may be hinting that you need to look after your physical health.

See also **ACCIDENT, DRIVING, JOURNEY**

Carnival

The carnival is a time when people traditionally forgets their worries and responsibilities, let their hair down, and enjoy themselves—a time when imagination and fantasy are allowed to run wild, when creative instincts, however unrealistic, can take precedence over mundane affairs. Being a participant in a dream carnival implies being willfully capricious and ignoring your responsibilities. If you are merely an onlooker, however, it may be that you have been feeling left out in your waking life. The dream may be telling you to make an effort to relax and let things be, rather than take the morally correct view all the time.

See also **MARKET, PROCESSION**

Carvings

Carvings or figurines in ivory or wood are often dream symbols of the collective unconscious, carrying the idea of ancient wisdom or, equally, of old religious beliefs with an outward appearance of wisdom, but lacking spiritual reality. Often a carving can be understood as a phallic symbol and may refer specifically to a sexual relationship the dreamer feels guilty about. There is usually a religious element to a carving, which represents something in the sense of "the old religion." The dreamer may be shown that the time has come to shed unquestioned beliefs and seek something more meaningful. Carvings or statues the dreamer recognizes may have a special meaning. Significance may lie in the detail of the carving or in the idea of carving or creating something tactile.

See also **STATUE**

A child may represent a young person or an emerging aspect of the self.

Cave

Connected with the abyss of materiality, as a cave in the Earth Mother, this symbol can imply a place of refuge or concealment. For a man, it can also represent motherhood and may point to the need for a young man to break away from his mother's dominating influence to gain true independence. In the sense of the abyss, a cave may represent an unseen and unknown danger. In this case it will probably refer to contents of the personal unconscious, as part of the dreamer's shadow.

See also **ABYSS, BASEMENT, DUNGEON, PIT, TUNNEL**

Chase

Being chased is a common dream experience. It is related to the idea of an unknown assailant—typically something you don't want to face up to in waking life. Perhaps you do not even want to identify it, but even when you sleep it will not leave you alone because it needs to be cleared up and expelled from your mind. In one of the earlier dream examples (Chapter 5), when the dreamer was being chased, the dream became lucid. The dreamer turned his pursuer around and made him run the other way. Amusing, perhaps, but this is not something to aim for!

You need to discover why you are being chased and who is doing the chasing. To achieve this, you need to let the chaser catch you. Only then will you identify and understand the problem, which has its roots in your own mind. When you wake after a dream of this nature, think through the characters and situations carefully and honestly: Part of you will not want to recognize the problem, but it needs to be confronted in your life.

See also **ESCAPING, FUGITIVE**

Child

A child may simply represent a young family member, but in cryptic dreams the innocent child usually represents the whole self or an aspect of the dreamer's personal contents, even though it will appear in the dream as someone else. When spiritual progress is taking place, the child symbol may represent the dawning of a formerly hidden aspect of the self that must now be assimilated.

See also **BABY**

Church

When interpreting the symbol of a church—as with any symbol with a hint of spirituality—bear in mind these two distinct possibilities. First, it may represent the possibility of further spiritual progress, the path of submission to a higher will. Second, it may indicate an ancient and possibly obsolete set of beliefs.

In the first case, the dream church will be seen as growing and flourishing. In the second, it may appear ruined, ivy-grown, abandoned, and crumbling. Both are fairly common features in dreams, and both are "good" symbols in that they represent the dawning of new understanding in the dreamer's waking mind. Spires and steeples may carry the same implications, as may more abstract church symbols, such as the sound of bells, singing, or chanting. To dream of entering a beautiful church and feeling at peace implies the dreamer's arrival at a new level of understanding. The full context of the dream and the lifestyle of the dreamer should be considered, of course. Unpleasant, disturbing dreams involving churches need urgent personal interpretation.

See also **ABBEY, ALTAR**

Cistern

A trough of water that can be emptied or flushed out: As a dream symbol this implies that you have been keeping your emotions—and probably your sexual desires—in check to a great extent. Perhaps you are becoming frigid; certainly bottled up to an undesirable degree. Empty the cistern and allow those emotions to flow!

See also **DAM, WATER**

Climbing

Two very distinct types of climbing occur in dreams – material and spiritual. On the material level, climbing implies ongoing effort and ambition aimed at achieving goals, especially at work—though it may reflect a difficult family situation: Marriage sometimes seems like a hard climb through life!

Spiritual climbing, on the other hand, is not connected with material success or comfort, but indicates that you are searching for a spiritual path that will satisfy your inner self. You may be climbing a dream mountain covered with ice and snow. This reflects the fact that you are going through a period of hardship or are about to enter a difficult phase in your life. If you reach the summit of a hill in your dreams, the rest of the journey should be downhill, and your difficulties will soon pass.

Finally, if you are clearly getting nowhere in your dream climb, and seem in danger of falling, the symbol is warning you to take a long, hard look at all aspects of your life, and to change direction in some major respect. Your ambitious sights may be set too high!

See also **LADDER, MOUNTAIN, OBSTACLES**

Clock

A symbolic timepiece points to triggers, opportunities, consequences, and fate. The clock face itself is a mandala, which can represent the dreamer's whole life. There comes a time in everybody's life when the alarm goes off and the fateful hour strikes; the dreamer should be advised when such a moment is imminent.

Two clocks together also have great significance in a dream. They represent two lines of destiny that have met in the space-time continuum—two people, perhaps—and this meeting point is the trigger for a new start, a new direction. The sundial is also a mandala of the self; it suggests a long, difficult life journey in the dreamer's past. With its gnomon and plinth, a sundial also carries phallic significance, and suggests that a change in lifestyle is imminent.

See also **CALENDAR, FALL, MANDALA**

Clothes

A most important symbol, clothes represent our sense of being, persona, or social facade, our passionate content, the way we think of ourselves, and the way others think of us. The symbol may refer to clothes worn by the dreamer or by someone else in the dream. Like an actor's costume, clothes sum up the nature of the character. In dreams, important people or nonpersonal principles and powers in the guise of people normally wear impressive robes.

Unknown quantities and suspicious circumstances may be represented by characters in shady, dark clothes. To dream that your own clothes are inadequate or not stylish enough or that you can never find the right outfit to wear implies that you do not feel able to fit in to the social scene—it means you are lacking in confidence. Success in many fields depends on confidence in your own ability to fill the role; if your clothes seem unsatisfactory in your dreams, you should be helped to put on the new clothes of confidence in waking life. Others tend to see you as you present yourself, hence the symbol; you are judged by appearance, which you largely project for yourself.

In more general terms your dreaming self can be aware of clothes that sum up the waking situation for you: A sick person may dream of a figure dressed in red, the color of blood; a widow may dream of a wedding in which the bride is dressed in black. A dream that involves clothes always calls for personal interpretation.

See also **FASHIONS, HAT, NAKED**

Clouds

By their nature, clouds are insubstantial and usually high above the ground. As a dream symbol, they conceal whatever unknown situation is or may be above the normal state of the dreamer. Clouds differ from fog or mist, which, as dream symbols, may conceal the future and hide what is at or below the status of the dreamer. Storm clouds carry the idea of conflict, though it may not directly involve the dreamer. To dream that someone else passes through clouds in some way implies that he or she has progressed to a state that cannot yet be known by the dreamer.

See also **FOG, MIST**

Corpse

To dream that an unknown person lies dead in surroundings familiar to you implies that something you once had is no longer available to you. If the surroundings in the dream are unfamiliar, it may be that someone you know is suffering the same sense of loss in real life. Of course, you may dream that someone

near and dear lies dead, but this may also mean that you have been worrying about this person and, perhaps, being overprotective.

See also **BURIAL, DEATH, FUNERAL**

Cow

Domestic cattle have symbolic significance in many cultures. The symbol of the cow is liable to emerge from the collective unconscious as representative of motherhood in the sense of a sustaining Mother Earth—the fertility goddess who appears in many guises. By inference, cows can represent the regularity or reliability of nature, the natural bounty of the earth, good harvests, and times of plenty.

See also **ANIMALS, BULL**

Crocodile

When they feature in your dream, creatures of this type—alligators or crocodiles, komodo dragons, giant lizards, dinosaurs—usually represent some set of emotions you probably thought were extinct, but that have merely lain dormant for a long time. You may perhaps look over a familiar wall in your dream and discover a swamp full of frightening creatures on the other side. They represent dark desires you thought were long gone, but that remain within your unconscious mind—part of the shadow. When you do something out of character and say, "I don't know what got into me!" most likely it was one of your dream crocodiles making its presence known.

See also **ALLIGATOR, DRAGON, MONSTER**

Crossroads

We use this idea in everyday life to suggest a moment of choice, a time when our direction may change, a crucial stage when we are forced to make a decision about our future course. As a dream symbol, crossroads suggest dubious behavior or criminality. Historically, in Europe, crossroads were often the places for meting out rough justice: Criminals were hanged and buried there. Sacrifices, too, were often made there in ancient times, so as a crossing point of fate, their atmosphere was full of doubt or hidden danger. There is also the story of meeting the devil at the crossroads and selling our soul in return for worldly goods.

On a more pleasant note, in some countries crossroads have been thought of as meeting places for entertainment, and inns or restaurants were often built there. So, besides a fateful choice that must be made, crossroads can carry the sense of a meeting between unrelated ideas.

See also JUNCTION

Crystals

If you feel attracted to various crystals in your dream, it may imply that you have been relying too heavily on the material things of life and seeking exclusively material solutions to your problems. Although many people believe that crystals have spiritual or healing power, they are still material objects, and any benefits they may bring will be of a material nature. Your dream may be telling you to start looking for a way to approach truly spiritual matters: to find out more about your soul life.

See also EARTH, JEWELS

Cup

A cup or chalice is a universal symbol of the collective unconscious, signifying preordained fate. In some cultures it may appear as a calabash, a drinking horn, or even a skull. To Christians it tends to represent something unpleasant that must be done as a duty and from which there is no escape. Jesus is said to have received the vision of a cup shortly before his arrest and crucifixion. In any culture it represents fate—an unavoidable circumstance that is about to descend on the dreamer. When the symbol takes the form of a bejeweled chalice of precious metal, it may well mean that something of great benefit to the dreamer is about to happen. It can also represent a feeling of divine approval of the dreamer's situation in waking life.

See also VASE

Dam

A great volume of water—the dream symbolism for emotions—is being held back by the strength of materiality, by determination. It may be that you are holding back your own feelings about some person or some circumstance: Perhaps you feel drawn to somebody but are unable to express your true feelings. The dream is not telling you what to do about the situation; it is merely pointing out that such a state of affairs exists. If the dam should burst, disaster may ensue, so waking wisdom is called for. Tread carefully around your emotional or sexual affairs; consider the possible consequences before you act.

See also CISTERN, WATER

Dance

Most dances involve two or more people, and a dream of dancing with someone is usually an expression of sexual desire. Organized or ritual dances are not limited to humans; before mating, many birds do courtship dances as well. Like birds, people tend to behave in accordance with the rules of human instincts. Solitary dances may be a simple expression of joy, but they may also imply that you have been concealing your true feelings. Line-dancing or folk dancing, with the dancers forming symmetrical patterns, may represent a mandala of the self.

See also **BALLET, MANDALA, THEATER**

Darkness

As a dream symbol, darkness describes the unknown part of the self, the personal unconscious waiting to be explored through dreams. In fog or mist your way forward is merely obscured or delayed. Darkness suggests ignorance of, or alienation from, higher states of consciousness rather than uncertainty. Dreams of walking through a dark tunnel without apparent end may be experienced during the night, but dawn dreams of darkness are more likely to involve a glimpse of light as if at the end of a tunnel. Darkness is not necessarily a "bad" symbol—rather a necessary and temporary stage along the route toward personal fulfillment.

See also **ECLIPSE, LOST, TUNNEL**

Death

In dreams the image of death need not necessarily refer to death of the physical body. Detailed dreams predicting physical death—unless they can be taken as a warning to take evasive action—should be accepted with equanimity as something we have no control over. Paradoxically, all spiritual progress proceeds by way of psychic death, for death is the necessary precursor of rebirth. We might even come to realize that the human soul, the nonegoistic self, also has to face a process akin to death and rebirth in order to change for the better. As a dream symbol, therefore, death may imply a change from the old to the new, from the tired and worn out to the new and progressive.

See also **BURIAL, CORPSE, DARKNESS, FUNERAL**

Demon

This is the archetype of the personal shadow: a representative of the contents of the personal unconscious, made up of the numerous ideas, impulses, and characteristics that have been rejected or not recognized by the conscious mind. All the features, faults, and failings of the subpersonality combine to create a symbolic figure that may assume many forms. It is liable to appear in dreams to haunt people who wish to seek spiritual contact. It is a part of the psyche, which seems *not* to want to come to awareness and, having taken on a will of its own, takes on a frightening guise in order to strengthen its own nature.

See also **ADVERSARY, WITCH**

Desert

To dream of traveling in the desert implies barrenness, either physically or spiritually. The symbol often reflects your own feelings about the way your life seems to be going. A dream situation where no plants grow reflects a sense of powerlessness, of being overwhelmed by events. Remember the world dream: You may obtain a seed, which will germinate and grow in your dream desert and transform it into an oasis. It is not impossible!

See also **SAND**

Dice

As a symbol of gambling or taking a chance, a dream involving dice could scarcely be clearer. But there is also a suggestion of the inevitability of fate and your own feeling of being swept along by the tide of events. Take note if the dice in your dream come up with a particular number or set of numbers, as they will relate to your own ideas and recent experiences. Only you will be able to decode these numbers and bring out their meaning. There is one proviso, however: To dream of the double six may be an example of wish fulfillment. If this is the case, and if you have been hoping for something that seems important to you, it may be a case of "in your dreams!"

See also **PLAYING**

Digging

Digging in a dream usually represents an attempt to uncover secrets of some sort. These secrets hidden beneath the ground probably make up the contents of your own unconscious mind. It is not usual to dream about uncovering the contents of *someone else's* unconscious mind—it is entirely a personal affair. On the other hand, the secrets being dug for may be some information or indication from the past that needs to be uncovered and brought into the light. Note carefully who is doing the digging. If not yourself, is it a friend, a relative, or a stranger? Try to recall your feelings during and immediately after the dream. Were they fearful, perhaps, or hopeful? It will be a personal dream that only you can decode successfully.

See also **ARCHAEOLOGY, PIT**

Dirt

Your dreaming self is well aware of the contaminating properties of dirt; but dreams involving something particularly unclean need personal interpretation. Does the dirt come from someone else, or is it already a feature of the personal unconscious? The dream is certain to express this clearly. It is natural for your personal shadow to contain all sorts of impurities that may not be acceptable to your waking mind. To become aware of this kind of dirt represents a cleansing process. Make an effort to identify the true nature of this dream dirt and to transform it into something positive.

See also **BUGS, EXCREMENT**

Diving

Taking the plunge is a well-known expression meaning to commit yourself to some course of action, and the dream symbol of water carries the clear meaning of deep emotions or powerful sexual feelings. Your dream of divers, or of diving into deep water yourself, will probably be based on these two meanings. Perhaps in real life you are committing yourself to a strongly emotional situation or entering a new emotional or sexual relationship and you are not at all sure of the outcome. The dream calls for caution. Do not commit too deeply or swim out of your depth in this involvement, whatever it may entail in real life.

See also **WATER**

Doctor

The doctor in your dreams will probably have arrived in response to some deep worry you have about your own or others' health. But it may not be merely physical well-being that is in question: The inner feelings dislike immorality, for instance, and may be warning you of moral ill health. If the dream doctor is a real-life doctor known to you personally, physical health will be the issue. If an archetype figure, your own wise man or father-advisor, the doctor is more likely to be offering you advice on your moral or spiritual health—the well-being of your own innermost self. Spiritual malaise is something very real that the personality tends to overlook—but your own feelings during and immediately after your doctor dream will give you a hint as to where your priorities should be.

See also **BLOOD, HOSPITAL, WISE PERSON**

Dog

For thousands of years dogs have appeared in dreams as symbols of the unconscious mind—or of the underworld. They represent the human animal nature well, because they live with us, apparently sharing our sense of social status, fitting in with our way of life. Canine instincts, or those of the wolf pack, often compare favorably with some of our own social customs. The personal shadow can take on the appearance of a dog in our dreams, letting its demonic nature be known only after it has been petted and accepted. When a clearing-out process has begun, the dream symbol of the dog eating its own vomit—thereby re-creating the material that makes up the personal shadow—is a warning against returning to former bad habits. In your own dream you will probably know if a dog is just a dog, or is a part of yourself. Interpretation is bound to be a personal matter.

See also **ANIMALS, DEMON, WOLF**

Dolphins / Porpoises

Seemingly carefree creatures of the deep, intelligent, full of fun, incredibly athletic, equally at home in rough seas and in calm, dolphins are friendly in the human sense but are also capable of all the less-than-human activities that characterize animal behavior, including aggression and cruelty as well as playfulness: All these qualities combine with dolphins' complete mastery of their environment—and in the dream, it is the water of deep emotions and sexual arousal. The dream may be suggesting that you see others better placed than yourself in the social scene, perhaps with jealousy or envy. Your dream may be advising you to test this metaphorical water gingerly and not to venture too far out at first. You may not, after all, get on very well with these dream creatures when you are in their environment and out of your depth.

See also **ANIMALS, WATER**

Door

Passing through a dream door symbolizes experiencing or becoming aware of a different level of being, and it appears in example dreams elsewhere in this book. As a dream symbol, a door may open to reveal light and is often associated with a near-death experience. The difference between a door and a gateway is that you can see through and around a dream gate; you know what lies beyond and merely wish to attain it. In the case of a door, whatever lies beyond is utterly unfamiliar and new. You do not as a rule know whether you want to go through it or not.

See also **GATEWAY**

Dragon

Interpretation of this symbol will depend almost entirely on your personal and cultural background. What does a dragon mean to you? What kind of dragon is it? What feelings does it invoke in you? If you have firm answers to any of these questions, you will probably be able to interpret its appearance in your dream. It may, however, be a denizen of the primeval swamp that is your personal unconscious. It may appear as the guardian of a mysterious cavern containing an unknown treasure—and this is also a part of yourself. Experience your own dragon and make a pet of it; you may then be shown the treasure.

See also **ALLIGATOR, CROCODILE, MONSTER, TREASURE**

Driving

For a person who habitually drives, as a dream symbol driving represents personal progress through life. In dream life the car is seen merely as an extension of the legs, and is unlikely to represent a substantial journey. For people who do not drive, riding a bus or train can also symbolize everyday progress through life. Driving a bus with passengers implies that the dreamer is, or feels, responsible for the welfare of others. A family man, for instance, might dream he is driving his family in a passenger vehicle. In such dreams the circumstances encountered along the route will need personal interpretation.

See also ACCIDENT, CAR, JOURNEY

Drowning

In dreams deep water symbolizes the depth of your emotions, including, very likely, your sexual feelings. If you are drowning in your own feelings or are unable to cope with your sexuality or your emotional attachments, you need to follow your dream through. Drown in the dream if you have to or scramble ashore, but on waking try to identify the nature of the water so that you are able to walk more safely around it in the future. You might even be able to find a bridge to cross in safety.

See also WATER

Duel

If you are arranging or fighting a duel with someone known to you in real life, the dream may be a straightforward reflection of some disagreement. But it may be that you thought you were in agreement with this person, and the quarrel is at the deepest level of your inner feelings. Your relationships need pondering very carefully. If you are dueling with an imaginary figure—possibly an archetypal character from your unconscious mind—you may be acting against your own conscience.

See also ADVERSARY, ASSAILANT

Dungeon

The dungeon is one of the many symbols of the personal unconscious mind, the repository for all the unacceptable thoughts and unwelcome emotions, unsolved problems, and personal worries that have troubled your thinking brain. This dungeon is a part of yourself, and everything locked in it also belongs to you. If in the dream you are shut inside yourself, perhaps you are shut in by your own passions in your everyday life.

If possible, you need to stand back within your own awareness and take an objective view of your own life. If you are quite honest with yourself, you will be able to see where your biggest problems are and what can best be done to alleviate them. Human desires can keep you locked up in a dream dungeon: They will never be completely satisfied and can impede your smooth progress through life!

See also BASEMENT, CAVE, PIT

Dust

It is not uncommon to dream that your familiar surroundings are coated with dust, sometimes to the extent that you can scarcely move or breathe. You may of course have experienced some traumatic incident that has triggered this dream. But if not, the symbol may be telling you that your daily routine needs a good airing. Dust is not the same as dirt, which tends to arrive from somewhere "out there." Dust is accumulated from within: perhaps from the scales of your own skin (are you becoming "hidebound"?) or from your own clothes (are you following a way of life

Dolphins are masters of their environment. How comfortable are you to join them?

Dreaming of an earthquake may reveal threats to material security or spiritual welfare.

that in some way clings to the past, refusing to accept new ideas and widely accepted principles?). Dream dust needs interpreting from your own point of view.

See also **BROOM, DIRT, EXCREMENT**

Eagle

Ever since recorded time began, the eagle and other large, high-flying birds of prey have symbolized power, nobility, exaltation, mastery of the air, supremacy over other creatures, strength, ferocity, fearlessness, powers of observation, and keenness of vision; in many countries these birds have acquired almost supernatural status. In northern lands, the eagle is thought of as typical of barren snowbound crags and bleak moors, a wild creature of equally wild weather, a harbinger of fierce storms and bitter conditions.

Whether all these qualities actually typify a real eagle is of course open to doubt. But in a dream it does indeed symbolize all these things and more: patriotism, vigilance, a love of natural grandeur, and a quest for broad landscapes, unspoiled wilderness, and unexplored territory. In the United States, the Bald Eagle symbolizes not only their own country but also the quality of being American.

Probably one of the earliest of dream symbols, the eagle boasts one of the most varied set of possible meanings; it is really up to the individual in each case to identify the dream eagle and isolate the real-life events around it and leading up to it.

See also **BIRDS**

Earth / Earth Mother

Representing the very beginning of the earthly creative process is the bare rock and soil from which sprang plants, then animals, and finally humans: the dark and gloomy king-dom of materiality into which—according to the ancient legend recorded by blind poet John Milton—the archangel Lucifer was "Hurled headlong flaming from th'ethereal sky" to rule over the material world. Small wonder, then, that archetypal earth symbols have arisen over the millennia, and comforting legends of a great Earth Mother nourishing us on her broad bosom, rearing us until we are mature enough to take our leave and make our own way beyond that "ethereal sky" to seek fresh universes and broader horizons. Comforting or frightening, such dream symbols serve to stir our spiritual awareness of life beyond that of our own solid world.

See also **GODDESS**

Earthquake

If you have experienced violent earthquakes yourself, your dream may simply be recalling your fears and the threat to your security. As a dream symbol, an earthquake expresses very clearly the shakiness of materiality when you are completely dependent on it. Materiality may sometimes seem to be all we have in life, but we have a duty also to look after our spiritual welfare. Faith can move mountains, the saying goes, and faith may be the missing factor in your life. On a smaller scale, a dream earthquake may express concerns about some organization, the place where you work, or your own family or financial security.

On a purely factual level, to dream of an earthquake may be warning you of violent and unpleasant consequences that may result from your current actions. If any people known to you are in the dream, this will provide a powerful clue as to the nature of the possible disruption, and you should be able to place the dream symbol where it belongs in your case.

See also **VOLCANO**

Eating

As a dream symbol, eating means that you or the person eating are taking in or imbibing the essential nature of whatever is being eaten. It may not necessarily be standard food—all kinds of things are dreamt of as being eaten, and the nature or characteristics of the food should be treated as a separate dream symbol to be decoded accordingly. A dream involving eating may be a warning that you are being influenced negatively by the dream food. Whatever characteristics you normally associate with the food need very careful consideration. The dream may also be a simple and straight-forward warning against habitually eating something that is proving bad for you.

See also **BREAD, FEAST, FOOD**

Echo

According to ancient Greek mythology, nymph-goddess Echo fell in love with the vain youth Narcissus. When she finally realized that he was interested in nobody except himself, she pined away until nothing was left of herself but her voice. Perhaps your dreams involving echoes reflect some of these emotions—emptiness, lack of self-worth, the hopelessness of pursing an unattainable goal, with the hint of egotism or selfishness on somebody's part. It could be that you are emulating or admiring the characteristics of someone to the exclusion of your own better judgment. Hearing echoes or entering an echoing valley in your dream implies that your efforts are being wasted, that the reply you hoped for will not be forthcoming.

Eclipse

This is a fairly straightforward dream symbol, but a clear distinction should be made between solar and lunar eclipses.

The sun as a symbol is connected with career prospects or financial affairs, so when the sun is occluded and loses its light or heat, it suggests that something you relied on for well-being, sustenance, or comfort is drawing to a close or is at least being withdrawn for a short while.

A lunar eclipse, on the other hand, is more specifically connected with the physical body and with romance. Perhaps the object of your desires has made it known that your feelings are not being reciprocated. If romance is not at the forefront of your interests, the symbol may be expressing your own fears about your physical health. The moon controls the flow of the tides, and also that of the bodily fluids and the monthly cycle of menstruation. An eclipse of the moon may carry the meaning of circulation problems, or an approaching menstrual pause.

See also **DARKNESS**

Eggs

A universal symbol of the potential for new birth, eggs have formed a major part of the creative process since animate life began. They represent the formative yin fertilized by the fountainhead of the yang. A dream egg contains within itself a new principle: Something is about to emerge, but what? That question can only be answered by the dreamer personally. To dream of smashed eggs implies that a hoped-for outcome will not be forth-coming. Eggs, too (like the whole of creation), are associated with the sexual impulse, and a sexual motive may be hidden within the symbol—a dream euphemism for certain egg-shaped erogenous zones of the human body—but there is sure to be more than one simple meaning in a dream featuring so ancient a symbol of life.

See also **EMBRYO**

Elephant

Powerful, ponderous, proud, persistent, primordial, strong on memory, hugely endowed—the elephant is a potent symbol of all these qualities. Often as a dream symbol an elephant represents officialdom or bureaucracy. A man worried about an ongoing income tax inspection recently dreamed that a dangerous-looking elephant had taken up a position outside his house and was peering in through the windows. Elephants can also symbolize strong sexual desires. Women, especially, may experience dreams of this nature.

See also **ANIMALS**

Embryo

This is a very clear symbol of a newly forming entity and something, tangible or not, that is taking shape, something you should be able to identify. Take careful note of your feelings during and immediately after this dream. Did your discovery of this embryo make you feel happy or apprehensive?

See also **EGGS**

Enemy

A dream adversary is the personification of a hidden part of your own character that is causing you problems. A dream assailant is someone or something outside yourself that is making trouble. A dream *enemy* comes midway between the two, and its identity will largely depend on your understanding of the term *enemy*. We have all heard of *the enemy within*; it may be a very true saying: It may be composed of your own fears and suspicions. Let the context of the dream tell you what the problem is, because plainly some defensive action seems to be required in real life.

See also **ADVERSARY, ASSAILANT, OPPONENT, XENOPHOBIA**

Envelope

A seemingly plain symbol of an unknown message of some sort, an envelope is a symbol that poses a question but offers no answer. If you are mailing the envelope in your dream, it reflects your own unanswered questions and your attempts to get at the truth.

See also **CROSSROADS, EXAMINATION**

Escaping

The general meaning of this symbol is all too clear. The question is: Why are you escaping, and what are you escaping from? It is not an uncommon dream experience to find yourself running away and hiding from something unpleasant. If you are going through a difficult phase in your everyday life, this will provide the clue. If there is a real-life situation you actually do need to escape from, study the dream very carefully to see if it offers any clues as to the best way to go about this. Or it may be that you have been working too hard or are feeling run down and need a vacation—to escape from routine for a while. But it sometimes happens—especially in older dreamers—that dreams of escaping do not apply to any material real-life situation, but reflect a longing to find some kind of spiritual path, something that will remove them from their material prison of the earth. If you think this may be the case with you, why not ask around for a few ideas? You never know what you may find!

See also **FUGITIVE**

Examination

Taking an examination in your dream carries with it the obvious implication of some sort of test you are facing in real life. Are you over-confident about some approaching situation? Do you need to appraise the situation more carefully before leaping in? Marriage may be the subject of your dream exam. There are so many tricky situations that may arise, but they are all situations that should be shared and need not involve the go-it-alone attitude that typifies an examination candidate. Perhaps you need to confide your problems and share your worries with your partner.

See also JUDGE

Excrement

Not quite the same as dirt, human excrement in a dream invariably symbolizes unwanted human characteristics, perhaps a part of your own shadow that may appear as an unpleasant character or vague nightmarish figure. In a dream that involves excrement, the original characteristic has stopped being merely unwelcome, frightening, or threatening and has become disgusting to your conscious, waking mind. It is time to get rid of it! In dreams of this nature, however, disposing of this filth is often problematic. It will not disappear down the drain as it should; it clings to what it touches. But at least this particular demon has presented itself in the dream in a form that is ready to be disposed of.

Upon waking, why not try a little self-analysis? What was there before the excrement appeared? Think about this unpleasant subject very carefully and if you can identify the substance in real life, you should be able to free yourself of it.

See also DIRT, DUST, TOILET

Facade

A facade is a false front, and its meaning is much the same in a dream as in real life: You are putting on a mask so others will think you, or something connected to you, are more important and more significant than you really are. Or the opposite: appearances are being dumbed down to suit whatever is to be appeased or impressed. Remember that a building in a dream often refers to a person in real life—often your own self. Thus a dream facade to a building can carry many possible meanings. There are almost endless possibilities involving this symbol. All of them need your personal interpretation.

See also ACTING, PAINTING, THEATER

Factory

The factory is a place where things are manufactured. In a dream they may be purely abstract, such as ideas or attitudes. This symbol represents the power of materiality itself—the "satanic force" that often seems to stand between people and their pursuit of higher things—their spiritual path through life. We could equally express it as the hub of society; your own attitude to the products of the dream factory equates with your attitude toward society and the world in general.

The dream factory may seem a highly desirable place where you could find equality, friends, and all the good things of life. Alternatively, the symbol may reflect your own lack of confidence, where you view life as *them vs. us*, and feel excluded from the factory and the mainstream of life. Were you working in this dream factory or standing outside looking in? If you were looking in, did you find it an attractive place or one to be avoided? The symbol offers a look into your own self.

See also MACHINERY

Fall / Autumn

Fall marks the end of warm sunshine, flowers, and greenery; all draw to a close in a brief spectacle of color. The comparison with the autumn of our years has always been inevitable, and is the most likely significance of this season when it features in your dream. Perhaps you no longer feel young and are looking ahead—gladly, resignedly, or with trepidation—to your own declining years. This of course is not necessarily bad. But it may not refer to age: To dream of a forest with falling leaves usually suggests that an easy phase of your life is drawing to a close. Look on it as the season of mellow fruitfulness, and take stock of the future.

See also **CLOCK, FOREST**

Falling

A very basic sensation, falling features often in dreams. Sometimes it happens to a sleeper without any apparent supporting dream. The image may correspond in a personal sense with the original plunge into materiality in the world dream. It always implies that a base or attitude of mind that you thought was secure is not as reliable as you believe. Frequently, as you feel the sensation of falling, you realize you are dreaming and wake yourself up. If it happens to you again, determine to stay asleep and experience the conclusion of the fall. In the dream world, the consequence of falling is already part of you, part of the self, so you are not really escaping anything by waking up prematurely. Experience it again, identify its nature, and you may be able to deal with it in real life.

See also **EARTH MOTHER, FEAR**

Farm

If your life involves farming, a dream farm may simply set the scene for your dream as a homey situation. But if, like the majority of people, you have no such connection, a farm can signify a place where things—usually animals and crops—are grown and nurtured. In the dream farm people or principles can be nurtured, eventually to be released upon maturity. A farm can symbolize you yourself at soul level, a hidden place where your own potential is developed. If an apparent stranger emerges from this dream farm, look at the person very closely. Think about this person's appearance and characteristics for hidden meanings: These may be an important part of yourself waiting to be acknowledged!

See also **ANIMALS, ZOO**

Fashions

Clothes are a common symbol for personality. The implication is that if you follow a particular fashion in a dream, you have probably been following a "fashion" in your personality. The dream symbol may refer to you personally or to someone else; it certainly implies that some special characteristic, often an affectation or exaggerated style, has become habitual for the person who wears it and exhibits it.

See also **CLOTHES, HAT**

Fear

Dreams involving fear are usually called nightmares, and they can be truly terrifying. The experience may have been triggered by a frightening outside event, but its real cause is most likely to lie within the dreamer's own psyche. The original nightmare was imagined to be a supernatural being from outside the self—a witch or night hag—who sat on the sleeper's chest and constricted breathing, causing the sensation of terror. Nowadays we speak of sleep paralysis (which featured in an example dream in Chapter 5), which can be very frightening when it happens during a lucid dream and the dreamer is prevented from waking up. The night hag can sometimes take the form of an animal, a large dog or a wild creature, sitting on the dreamer and threatening to bite. Fear experienced by the dreamer is usually associated with a deep feeling of guilt, more often than not connected with sexual desires. A terrifying dream creature can sometimes be identified and given a name: Lust!

See also **ASSAILANT, PARALYSIS, XENOPHOBIA**

Feast

A feast implies overindulgence or extravagance. The meaning of this as a dream symbol depends largely on your own feelings during or immediately after the dream: If you felt any guilt, perhaps you are being greedy or selfish about something (not necessarily food) that would be better shared. However, if you felt quite happy about the feasting, especially if you were not alone, it may be that you are in for good fortune—not necessarily financial—a happy occasion, perhaps involving a forthcoming family gathering.

See also **BREAD, FOOD**

Feet

Feet are a potent symbol of your own or others' journey through life, and the ability or inability to progress spiritually. To dream that feet are missing or deformed may imply that your own willful nature is impeding the long march toward psychic wholeness. To understand this symbol is to become aware that a

journey really is necessary: Waste no more time! Start remembering and recording your dreams and heeding their message. Become aware also that you must not impede the progress of others by trampling on them or kicking them. Live and let live! Wheels may carry much the same significance in a personal dream.

See also **LAMENESS, PATH, ROAD**

Fence

A fence is an obvious symbol for a barrier, whether material physical, mental, psychological, or spiritual. It may be a moral boundary that you ought not cross. It does not bear quite the same significance as a dream wall or solid-panel fence that you cannot see through: You can normally see through a fence; you can "see" what the future holds, what you are missing, or what features you are unable to reach. It may be that your dream fence has fallen or been blown down. In this case, although the dream itself may have been triggered by, for example, a real-life gale, the symbolic significance is that a barrier that existed for you—whether physical, social, or work-related—has now been removed, and your way ahead is clear.

See also **WALL**

Fish / Fishing

The collective unconscious has often been symbolized by the image of the sea: broad, deep, and largely unexplored. The creatures that live in it are products of the collective mind, the desires, hopes, and fears of us all during the long human history. But the sea can also symbolize individual emotions and the sexual impulse; so can a gently running stream—a trout-filled brook perhaps, containing your own personal "fish," the unspoken objects of all your past desires and deepest feelings. So ancient a symbol calls for an investigation of our ancestral roots if we are to explore these hidden depths, but our dreams represent a "royal road to the unconscious mind," as Freud expressed it.

The dream symbol of you or another person fishing carries the implication of exploring the psychological and spiritual contents of the self. It represents your own desire to uncover what lies hidden within, and by so doing to set out on an exciting voyage of discovery.

See also **ANIMALS, SEA, WATER**

Flower

The symbol of a flower is related to the archetype of the persona—your social facade. It can represent something that is being presented, the qualities that you are intended to see and experience regarding something or someone; also the way you want others to see you. The flower—especially a four- or five-petaled flower—can also symbolize the self, particularly when it is displayed full-face in the manner of a mandala. However, a flower that is set on a surface, as a water lily floating on a pond, can symbolize the upper, conscious part of the self, above the dark contents of the unconscious mind. Strange or exotic flowers can represent an unusual encounter you have had, perhaps an unfamiliar religious experience. Flowers can represent the spiritual essence of the plant world, and may reflect the world dream. Dreams of an afterlife frequently feature flowery meadows and gardens.

See also **FOREST, LILIES, MANDALA**

Flying

The inner feelings are emotions below the horizon of consciousness—feelings that do not normally come to waking awareness, though they are filled with matters that most concern you. When they do come to your awareness, usually in dreams, they do not feel themselves to be encumbered with the physical body, and there is nothing to stop them flying or floating freely. Aware of all your hidden potentials, they often draw the distinction in dreams between your outer and inner emotions by personifying them. You may see yourself as two people: one earthbound and heavy, perhaps with characteristics you do not care to call your own; the other able to float and fly, with ideal characteristics. This latter person is the nonmaterial part of you.

See also **GLIDERS**

Fog

Doubt, not knowing what the future may bring, and uncertainty over the best path to take: All these negative feelings are symbolized by fog or mist. If we visit that great valley of materiality in our dreams, it will very likely be filled with fog, implying that spiritual light and wisdom are hidden from view. Experiencing fog in your dream does not imply that things will not improve for you; it simply means that a veil has been drawn over the future.

See also **CLOUDS, MIST, VALLEY**

Food

All influences, pieces of information, even thoughts and feelings, are as food to the psyche. As a result they may be represented as food in dream imagery, and there are virtually endless permutations of possible meanings.

Religious imagery, too, is full of references to spiritual food. But practical dreams of food—especially when you dream you are eating disagreeable or stale food—can have a purely practical meaning: You may quite inadvertently be eating stale or rancid material (for example, food past its sell-by date, or fat refried again and again) that is doing you physical harm.

See also **BREAD, FEAST, FRUIT**

Ford

Water symbolizes the emotions or the sex drive in dream imagery. You can use a ford as a way "across" the emotions or sex drive without running the risk of drowning or getting washed away—that is, of being overpowered by these psychological forces. If you are following a spiritual path, the symbol of a river is a very important one, since you will sooner or later need to cross over this potent stream of life forces to separate yourself and become independent of their power.

See also **PATH, ROAD, WATER**

Foreigners

As a dream symbol, "foreigners" signify almost any characteristic that you feel to be foreign to yourself. Your own feelings during the dream and your emotions on waking will provide the clue.

See also **CLOTHES, UNIFORM, XENOPHOBIA**

Forest

In dreams, a forest you are walking through usually symbolizes the thoughts and the workings of your own brain. This is true particularly when your preconceptions are holding you back or limiting your chances in some way. We tend to have fixed ideas that prevent us from advancing in life. The minds of even great men and women are sometimes so powerful, they become scornful of matters they consider illogical, religious, or spiritual. Sometimes we need to relax our thoughts and seek higher things, and this is when the forest features most strongly in our dreams.

In the great world dream the forest also represents the plant world and is therefore associated with aggression and intolerance. As with most dream symbols, practical interpretations should not be overlooked: If you have lived and worked in real-life forests, a dream forest may symbolize your own history and lifestyle.

See also **FALL, LOST**

Fortress

Are you outside your dream fort trying to get in, or are you safely inside? The power of authority, domination, self-containment; defense, protection, security, refuge, exclusion, discrimination, prejudice, favoritism—any one or more of these concepts could form the walls of your dream fortress. And whatever the feeling behind the image, its implication is that you, the dreamer, have not been feeling very companionable or comfortable with your surroundings—socially, at work, or in the family.

As with most dreams, the one best placed to decode its full meaning is the dreamer. Write down all the details and think about them; recall your feelings at the time and immediately afterward. Did anybody known to you play a part in the dream? If you can identify your fortress, you might wish to start dismantling its walls in real life by aiming to be neither an outsider nor an insider.

See also **BATTLEMENTS**

Fossils

Because fossils are a hint of ancient beings that once lived but are now apparently lifeless, dreams featuring fossilized remains are probably triggered by recent events in the dreamer's life, but the hint of past influences long gone from the awareness but still remembered in the background of consciousness remains. Dreaming of ancient things often means that something significant has arisen from the dreamer's own unconscious mind. Matters that seem long forgotten never really disappear and through dreams their influence on the personal unconscious is liable to reappear.

See also **ANTIQUE, ARCHAEOLOGY**

Fountain

This ancient symbol signifies something new coming to the awareness. The source of abstract properties could be learning, new understanding, new knowledge; spiritual experience, perhaps; hope or reassurance; "the fountain of life"—new birth or new scientific discoveries; "the fountain of youth"—acquiring a new lease on life or relief from physical ailments; new emotional experiences, new sexual adventures; newly acquired access to art or music. The dreamer will probably know which description applies.

See also **WATER**

Frost

Water in the atmosphere symbolizes the emotions you encounter all around you. When water vapor or dew freezes, frost appears; these emotions have become distinctly cold.

The symbol suggests that you have been feeling excluded from sympathy or from the reassuring emotional response you expected. There is a frosty patch, a difficult or slippery or unfriendly spell to surmount. Feelings tend to be reciprocal; possibly you have been withdrawn or isolated for some reason, and are experiencing the inevitable outcome of this. A change in attitude may be called for—though of course this is far easier said than done.

See also **GLACIER, JOURNEY, MOUNTAIN, SNOW** *and* **ICE**

Fruit

The outcome of any enterprise or hopeful effort may be symbolized as fruit. The type of fruit will depend largely on the dreamer's association of ideas. For example, a tamarind may symbolize good health in the East, but would be quite incomprehensible in the West. To Westerners, pears are frequently used by the dreaming self to represent bodily health. They can also represent the dreamer's own children. When the fruit is ripe and luscious, the omen is favorable; when it is shriveled or rotten it implies disappointing results. Grapes and cherries in particular may indicate sexual attraction, and the phallic implication is fairly obvious when bananas and similar shaped fruit and vegetables are involved.

See also **FOOD**

Fugitive

The dream of the outsider who would dearly like to be admitted to a more comfortable situation in life—or a dream that you yourself are hiding, afraid of capture, or longing to rejoin a community—is a powerful symbol expressing a burning desire to experience a more rewarding lifestyle: a breakthrough. If a possibility of this approaches, dreams often carry an impression of the fugitive, watching and waiting or gazing wistfully, like a lonely child.

See also **ESCAPING**

Funeral

Waking thoughts of death will often produce the dream symbol of a funeral, but it is not necessarily a symbol to be taken literally. It always implies the possible end of some circumstance. Old-fashioned dream books usually assert that a funeral portends happiness to come—the end of a bad period and rebirth into a better one. Personal interpretation will usually decide if this is the case. When thoughts of death are on your mind, the details of a dream funeral can carry significance. It happens quite often that what appears to be an actual funeral turns out to be only a sort of dress rehearsal of the ceremony, indicating imminent recovery from a life-threatening condition.

See also **BURIAL, DEATH**

Gateway

Allied to the symbol of a forest, a gateway leading from the trees into the open symbolizes a way of attainment, of escaping from the restrictions of thought, and possible entry into a higher mode of understanding. A gateway expresses the need for a new intellectual approach in any field of experience. It may be significant whether the dreamer actually passes through the dream gate, merely looks through it, or is no more than aware of its presence nearby. A door has a similar significance, but is usually a more inward symbol. Where the gate refers to a new way of thinking and receiving impressions, a door implies entry into a different dimension—often associated with an afterlife experience.

See also **DOOR, FENCE, WALL**

Ghost

This nebulous dream figure may be acting the role of unknown adversary—a part of your own self that you do not wish to know, and which you are rather afraid of. Sometimes it represents a similarly unpleasant feature connected with a member of your family—a "skeleton in the closet" that is never discussed and that would cause distress if it became public. In rare instances the dream ghost may not be frightening but happy and welcoming, in which case the hidden characteristic it represents may not be so bad after all. This is a very personal symbol of something known to exist but not openly acknowledged.

See also **ADVERSARY, DEMON**

Gift

An unexpected present is the fairly plain symbol of anything desirable that has been received from somebody else—not necessarily a material gift, but as often as not a new outlook, a new possibility for you. Sometimes the dream gift, when unwrapped, may be disappointing or not as pleasant as you had hoped. If you are presenting the gift to other people, there is probably an element of wish fulfillment in the dream: You may long to be well thought of (and don't we all?), but your efforts may not always be appreciated. It can only be a personal dream symbol, to be decoded on a personal basis.

See also **TREASURE**

Glacier

A solid river of ice winding though mountains can be telling you that your lifestyle is too

Luscious, ripe fruit symbolizes positive outcomes.

materialistic and your feelings have become trapped, telling you your life should be more than your present course of struggle suggests. Your feelings long to soar freely, but perhaps your pursuit of material goals has become more important to you than what you perceive as profitless emotions. Re-examine your lifestyle and try to devise a means whereby your feelings can be free. A more sincerely religious outlook may prove helpful.

See also **FROST, MOUNTAIN, SNOW** and **ICE**

Gliders

Relate this to the previous symbol of the glacier. This suggests that feelings that were trapped are now flying freely, soaring over the mundane level of existence below. The inner feelings that assemble our dream symbols can fly where they will, creating the sights or sensations of flying, floating, or gliding through the air. A glider may be independent and free, but it is still bound by the elements—restricted by the hard facts of life on earth. This is frequently a wish-fulfillment dream, allowing the emotions to escape briefly from their bonds of society, family, and work.

See also **FLYING**

Goddess

The Earth Mother, or a figure perceived as a goddess, is one of the archetypes of the collective unconscious, normally occupying for a woman the same position as a king or hero figure does for a man. She may offer sound advice when needed. As a passive figure, the great Earth Mother may appear to either sex as a dream symbol expressing a first inkling of

the reality of the world dream—as in the example dream at the beginning of Chapter 3.

On a more personal level, the symbol represents a personification of female confidence and strength. It implies caring for others. When this is overdone it can indicate a domineering tendency best avoided.

See also **EARTH, WISE PERSON, WITCH**

Gold

As a symbol, gold has two different extremes of meaning. The common denominator is its great value. Gold can symbolize the material wealth of the earth, which, in religious terms, is to be found within the satanic realm. It can also symbolize spiritual wealth. Golden garments may symbolize great authority on earth and respect, or the divine authority of angels, or the attainment of a truly spiritual path. The dream image of gold, therefore, as old-fashioned dream books often assert, can suggest that undue attachment to material gain may result in long-term loss and disappointment; it may equally refer to the achievement of some sort of enlightenment.

See also **DRAGON, TREASURE**

Gorge

As a dream symbol, a rocky gorge, ravine, or rift in the rocks expresses the idea of entering or penetrating material solidity. Some religious people may have an image of the Rock of Ages in which they can hide, but even this is a material, not a spiritual, image.

The symbol is more likely to represent a lack of security; a fear of falling into that gaping ravine, because the strength or reliability of the material world is not as secure as you had expected. It can appear when you are threatened with loss of job security or when family split-ups are imminent. It can also symbolize the personal unconscious mind yielding up some of its secrets, or the feminine nature, the yin, of the psyche threatening to swallow up the personality, which feels inadequate or insecure. As a dream symbol, a rocky gorge may be warning you to look more openheartedly on your associates; on the other hand, someone known to you may be exerting an unwelcome influence, and the time may have come to back away from a situation that has become threatening.

See also **ABYSS**

Grave

As a symbol of death, this may carry a straightforward message regarding a funeral, past or forthcoming. More likely, though, it is pointing out the final outcome of a situation—a dead-end venture, perhaps, you are being led into. A grave can also symbolize something you once felt strongly about but are now able to forget. In more general terms, it can represent the unconscious mind and its hidden contents: Perhaps there is something in your past life that now needs revealing. Equally, it may be something that has outrun its usefulness and needs finally putting to rest.

See also **BURIAL, DEATH, FUNERAL**

Hat

If someone has more than one job or interest, we say he wears many hats. The dream symbol is similar: It identifies the person wearing the hat, the function this person represents; and also how he or she wants to be seen. Archetypes of the unconscious mind are often to be identified by their hats. Where the dream subject is feminine and the hat, or lack of it, seems important, remember that in many cultures women are considered wanton or immoral if they go hatless in public. It can therefore symbolize virtue and morality.

See also **CLOTHES, FASHIONS**

Hedge

A real-life hedge is rather like a small strip of woodland that forms a protective home for small animals and birds; as a living boundary, it can keep large animals and humans confined or excluded; it can mark where one type of environment finishes and another begins; it can mark the course of a path or road or a labyrinth which may be difficult to escape. A dream hedge can be menacing or friendly, a help or a hindrance; it can bear thorns as well as fruit or flowers; the world dream points out that plants can be aggressive and warlike. In your dream there will probably be no doubt about the role the hedge is playing.

See also **FENCE, WALL**

Hero

This is an archetype of the unconscious mind, related to the image of the wise old man and the king. In dreams the hero usually symbolizes a part of the self that occupies the highest position in your personal mandala: the antithesis of the personal shadow, and the principle that opposes it in dreams. The female equivalent is the goddess—the wise woman who gives advice—and she, too, could feature in dreams as a heroine. Hero or heroine, this image includes everything in your own psyche that you consider to be admirable, brave, and

A goddess is an archetypal dream figure symbolizing wisdom, strength, and guidance.

reliable. Superman, Batman, Superwoman, and similar characters are cartoon projections of the symbolic hero in all of us.

See also GODDESS, KING, WISE PERSON

Holly

In dreams holly usually carries the same meaning as thorns—a thorny set of problems that are likely to accompany a certain course of action, but with the added dimension of beauty or festivity. In real life some situations may look pleasant or promising—they may appear as something inviting and reliable, that is, but your inner feelings tell you they involve risks or have certain inborn dangers; it is a cautionary symbol.

See also THORNS

Honey

An ancient dream symbol, the product of a beehive or a wild bees' nest, honey has always been greatly valued as a luxury food to be obtained at some personal risk. If there is an attractive real-life situation in the forefront of your mind or if you are considering some new and promising enterprise, this could be the *honey*: The rewards may be great, but the dream is warning you to be careful. Of course, honey is also used as an affectionate name for a person—so the dream symbol of honey in a familiar form may be a representation of that person in your feelings.

See also FOOD

Horse

If you are connected with horses in real life, your dream horse may merely have a practical meaning for you. Otherwise, a horse featuring in dreams often represents your own sexuality, or that of a husband or child. In the world of nature, the horse is a competitive and moral animal; a trained horse retains its competitive nature (as a racehorse, for instance) and is normally submissive and modest. In dreams, a white horse often symbolizes a person known to you and whose sexuality you are nervous about, but someone you trust anyway.

A black horse represents an unknown quality of animal passion, and may symbolize the sexuality of a person whom you find alarming. The mythical unicorn is a closely related symbol, and this may be seen as a horse that bears something of a spiritual status besides obvious sexuality. In all cases the symbol of a horse or horselike creature has powerful emotional overtones.

See also ANIMALS, YOKE

Hospital

While we can recognize this as being the place to be cured—or at least to be patched up or treated for some ailment—in the case of a dream hospital, the injury or illness is likely to be connected to the psyche rather than the body. It will be in the mind or emotions or will be a malaise of the soul. If you are given any clues in the dream involving people whom you know or places that are familiar to you, think about them carefully. Your dream hospital is pointing out that something may be of great benefit to you.

See also DOCTOR

Hotel

As a dream symbol, a hotel represents any set of circumstances you seem to be relying on—not necessarily a solidly real place; it could just as well be a family situation, a circle of friends, or organization you are associated with. You are being "looked after" in some way. A fairly common dream involves leaving a hotel where you have been staying, walking away, and getting lost in unfamiliar streets. Take this as a warning not to reject, neglect, or abandon a situation that has been beneficial to you; it may result in losing your direction in life. You will usually be able to identify the dream hotel with something important in real life.

Hurricane

A great storm, gale, or typhoon all cause immense disruption of the elements in real life. A dream hurricane expresses and sometimes predicts an equally traumatic shake-up in the dreamer's life, usually affecting the feelings or peace of mind. Frequently, the symbol refers to public reactions to something closely involving the dreamer. This dream symbol is more often experienced by celebrities and figures in the public eye than the rest of the population. The shake-up to be experienced may refer to an inner, emotional, or even spiritual trauma.

See also **BAMBOO, EARTHQUAKE, TIDAL WAVE, VOLCANO**

Idol

This somewhat primitive religious symbol can mean different things to different people. It is a question of individual understanding. When it forms the nub of a seemingly important major dream, especially a dawn dream, it needs considering very thoroughly and sincerely. If this was your dream, what is your own religious understanding and what were your feelings during the dream? Where do you stand in relation to the spiritual dimension? The dream may be recording an important

step up for the psyche or, perhaps, a letdown. If the former, follow your ideas about this idol and decide what it means to you: An idol represents or symbolizes a principle that is greater than either itself or its worshippers. If the latter, you probably already know the nature of this dream idol; take notice.

See also **STATUE**

Incense

When you follow a spiritual path, as distinct from a religious one, you may experience *ethereal incense*—a nonphysical smell that arises when coarse materialistic characteristics are expelled from inner feelings. Thousands of years ago people tried to recapture this folk memory experience by burning fragrant substances that recalled the ethereal smell. They made it a part of their religious practices. Wishful thinking, perhaps; but it showed sincerity and faith, and these are the characteristics being expressed in a dream that involves incense. Whatever is associated with the incense in the dream is something to be valued and respected.

See also **CHURCH**

Jetty

A landing stage, a pier, a breakwater—any structure that extends into the sea—symbolizes that you are approaching an emotional (or perhaps sexual) situation, and observing it or making use of it without actually becoming involved. It may be that a wave is threatening to wash you off the jetty. The implication is that you are set to become deeply involved and possibly swept out of your depth. The actual nature of the sea and the jetty will be matters for you to resolve personally.

See also **WATER**

Jewels

A chest of jewels or similar treasure of great value tends to feature in dreams investigated by psychoanalysts and is interpreted in various ways. Unlike gold, jewels almost inevitably symbolize good things that come by way of materialistic rather than spiritual pursuits. As a rule, dreams in which they appear need to be analyzed on a personal basis.

See also **CRYSTALS, GOLD, PEARL, TREASURE**

Journey

Your symbolic dream-journey may refer to a journey of the mind or a new emotional experience. It may also refer to your normal progress through life, recording your experiences on the way or hinting at experiences yet to come. Your relationship with others and your personal health are items likely to be symbolized during this sort of dream. Try to decode the whole picture—it will most likely prove to be highly significant in your waking life.

See also **CAR, FEET, PATH, RAIL TRIP, ROAD**

Judge

The religious advice to "judge not that ye be not judged" should be taken seriously. In a dream you may be the judge or you may be the one receiving judgment; in either case the dream is pointing out that the ultimate judge is your own conscience—your own soul—which is why nobody can escape judgment in the long run. The dream symbol seems to be telling you to search your own conscience and try to put right anything you may have done wrong—and this is not always easy advice to follow!

See also **ANGEL, EXAMINATION**

Junction

Like a crossroads in the journey of life, the dream symbol of a highway or rail junction shows that you have a choice of directions; you probably know what those choices are in your waking life. It may be that fate will lend a hand and make the choice for you—in which case you have no option but to experience the change of direction as it happens and accept whatever the change may entail. Instead of trying to make a hard decision, a more submissive attitude might be helpful in your journey through life.

See also **CROSSROADS**

King

As a male archetype related to the hero and the wise old man, the king symbolizes the part of the psyche that is seen as the seat of wisdom and accumulated knowledge. In a woman's dreams, a kinglike figure may be the animus, or father figure. The king's exalted place for a woman is usually taken by the dream figure of a wise goddess or the Earth Mother.

See also **HERO, WISE PERSON**

Labyrinth

Here we have a variant on the dream of being lost, with one important difference: You know where you are in a labyrinth. Furthermore, you know where you want to go; so your only problem is finding the best way out. There are so many situations in life where it seems as if fate has lured you into a labyrinth, a maze set to impede your progress through life. It suggests a catch-22 situation, where every possible solution sets up a new problem. A dream labyrinth may be set to any scale—it may represent a comparatively minor or temporary problem at work or in close relationships, or it may reflect your entire life pattern. In either case, the dream itself is unlikely to offer a solution—only time will provide that; it is merely pointing out the tricky situation in which you find yourself.

See also **LOST**

Ladder

In the biblical account Jacob dreamed of a ladder reaching from earth to heaven. If something similar is in your dream, you probably know what it is telling you. More likely, however, it is pointing out a practical solution to an everyday, annoying problem. As a dream symbol, a ladder is most likely to appear before someone who has been feeling put upon. All the details of your dream need assembling and examining very carefully for clues. The dream is certainly showing you a possible means of escape from your own limiting lifestyle—a way of pulling yourself up by your bootstraps.

A dream building often represents yourself; it follows that a ladder reaching an upper story implies that you have been given a chance to gain a much higher and previously unknown region of your own psyche. Make the most of it in real life!

See also **CLIMBING, ESCAPING**

Lake

A dream lake, especially one that is dark and mysterious, is likely to be an allegorical picture of yourself. You cannot guess how deep the water is—there may even be monsters lurking in its depths. Occasionally, living creatures may disturb the surface—these are thoughts, impressions, feelings of guilt or unease, ideas that have disturbed you, or past incidents that your conscious mind has perhaps forgotten but that still live on in your personal lake of the unconscious, to be mulled over by the inner feelings. The surface of the lake represents your conscious emotions; whatever in the dream is sailing or swimming or floating or growing there can be related to your own recent feelings. You have probably been thinking deeply and feeling emotional about some issue or person: In effect, you have been looking down on your lake from the intellectual heights of the hills around you.

See also **WATER**

Lameness

Feet represent your journey in the world. This may be taken literally and refer to your everyday, physical progress; it may also refer to your more important spiritual journey through life. Something in your recent experience will probably have triggered a dream involving lameness. Is it you or is someone else in the dream lame? As a dream symbol, it points to a problem but offers no solution—the rest of the dream may hold significance. To your waking mind it may seem trivial when compared with the alarming prospect of real lameness; recall every detail of the dream and think about it carefully. It may be that you are in contact with people whom you watch enviously as they travel apparently without effort through their successful lives—but do you really want to be like them?

See also **FEET, JOURNEY**

Laundry

Soiled clothes are usually a symbol of guilty feelings—the clothes themselves represent your outward personality and the dirt is how

A king personifies wisdom and knowledge

you see your own (or someone else's) character, when this seems less than ideal. Soiled sheets or bedcovers (if they do not refer to any real-life situation) transfer your feelings of guilt to the bed and the bedroom.

See also **CLOTHES, DIRT**

Library

A collection of books is a source of knowledge. When this dream symbol appears, its interpretation depends largely on your own attitude toward books and what they mean to you. This can vary from gossip, fashion, and escapism to the idea of near-unattainable wisdom. Changing your library book in a dream implies that you are rejecting or are likely soon to reject your current lifestyle, your set of attitudes or perhaps the set of people you associate with and to start looking for something more rewarding in your life.

See also **BOOKS**

Lilies

These noble flowers tend to be associated with funerals and so with death; to dream of them can mean that you have been worrying about your own or another's health. But they are also symbolic of purity—wholesome aspirations or moral innocence. The name *Madonna lily* emphasizes this association with purity, especially in the physical sense of virginity. Water lilies, on the other hand, draw attention to whatever lies beneath them. They may represent the fabled lotus flower of clear consciousness—a misleading flower that floats over the unknown depths from where the plants are drawing their nourishment. The dream water lily, once again, is a symbol of the unconscious mind, with all its unseen contents.

See also **FLOWER, FUNERAL, WATER**

Lost

It is quite common to dream of being lost. You may be walking in the dream along a familiar route then suddenly lose your sense of direction and forget where you have to go or where you came from. Suddenly, everything seems unfamiliar—or *almost* familiar. You may find yourself in a place well known to you as a child. You may think about going home, only to realize that home is not there anymore. Dreams involving dying or the premonition of death often include this aspect. The symbol draws your attention to the fact that there is more than one dimension to life and that your spiritual side should be awake and able to find the right direction. Even on the most mundane level, the symbol can imply that you have lost direction in your professional or family life.

See also **LABYRINTH, UNEMPLOYED**

Machinery

This is a basic symbol of materiality, representing the whole world of civilization, industry, and commerce, but seen from your own personal viewpoint. If you have recently been feeling isolated from the practical workaday world, you may dream perhaps of a factory where you are watching and listening to the whining and humming of great machines with some apprehension. The dream implies that you have in some way drawn apart from the world of turmoil, and this may be a good thing: It is after all what sages have tried to do in all ages past, in the quest to find the true self.

See also **FACTORY**

Mandala

The mandala, from the Sanskrit word, is a "magic circle," a symbol of the self. In dreams this can take many forms besides a mere diagram on a piece of paper. It can be represented by a folk dance in which the participants form a square or circle; by a city square with trees and people, perhaps seen from above; by an ancient stone circle; by a garden; by a flower; by almost any symmetrical arrangement, in fact, often with a clearly identifiable center and four corners. Dream symbols such as this call for sympathetic assistance in personal interpretation. They imply progress in a psychological or even deeper sense. When the self is seen in symbolic form, it may imply a growing awareness of the possibility of genuine spiritual contact, to begin a journey along your own spiritual path.

See also **CLOCK, FLOWER**

Market

A dream symbol indicating the hubbub or hurly-burly of life, the market represents the point at which you interact with other people. We cannot really do without it, but we ought not to let it occupy all our waking minds. Most people could do with less of it; a few could do with more—it is all a matter of balance. To decode this symbol you need to reexperience the feelings you experienced during the dream and uncover your own attitude toward the marketplace society. Sometimes we all need to draw away from others for a while and rediscover our true selves.

See also **CARNIVAL, PLAYING**

Mist

You have arrived at a time and place in life where you cannot see the way ahead at all clearly: This is exactly what a dream mist implies—past certainties have disappeared and doubt has crept in. This could well represent a major turning point in your life, promising a completely new direction, a new course, and a new outlook. This may baffle your mind, but your way ahead is still there, if only you could see it, mapped out for you by fate. Patience is called for on your part, so be careful not to rush into new enterprises or liaisons. Wait until the outcome is clear before making important decisions.

See also **CLOUDS, FOG, VALLEY**

Monster

It sometimes happens that you deliberately avoid doing something you would enjoy but think you ought not do. You may have an interest that you would rather no one knew about; something you thought belonged safely to your past may stir in you again. Any of these things may be symbolized in your dreams as a monster or a creature like a crocodile crawling out of a primeval swamp. It belongs to the topmost part of the shadow, a part that can quite easily crawl upward into your conscious life at any time. The best plan is to identify this monster, draw it from its swamp, look at it, appraise it, and come to terms with it. Picture it as something small that you can hold in the palm of your hand and it may then no longer worry you.

See also **ADVERSARY, ALLIGATOR, CROCODILE, DRAGON**

Monument

In waking life a monument usually expresses determination not to forget something that affected us deeply. It implies a sense of solidity. Some monuments may signify little more than an outward display of power, pride, or wealth.

Inner monuments that appear in dreams express things that affect us deeply in a more personal sense, though they, too, may be projections of power, pride, and wealth. Traditionally dream monuments have been regarded as expressions of sex—as phallic symbols—but this applies far less often in today's anything-goes society, where surface values tend to take precedence over the deeper issues of life. A dream monument is likely to represent something private that has affected you very deeply but which you do not care to formulate or put into words.

See also **IDOL, STATUE**

Mountain

Any barrier—real or imaginary, physical or psychological—may appear symbolized in dreams as a mountain, a mountain range, or a cliff face that needs to be scaled. The same symbol may also represent not a barrier but new heights that you feel need to be conquered. Depending on your own attitude and development, a mountain may represent the spiritual heights of sainthood or the satanic heights of materiality. To dream of walking over a mountain or a hilltop implies an awareness of hard, slow progress through life currently being experienced, with the promise of an improved—downhill—situation later on.

See also **CLIMBING, PATH**

Mud

Walking through mud in a dream seems to imply that things have not been going too well for you in real life. Symbolically, water represents feelings—emotions and sexual desires. Earth represents materiality—day-to-day reality, money, work, and ordinary social life. A surfeit of water mixed with earth makes mud. A surfeit of desires and unrestrained feel-ings mixed with your social and business life makes trouble: Your progress through life can become difficult. Wading through mud in your dream can imply that your social or work relationships are going through a sticky patch and your own attitude could be to blame!

See also **DIRT, SWAMP**

Museum

The museum is a symbol of ancient artifacts and ideas that are no longer relevant yet remain respected or admired. An actual museum is a place where you are expected to be well behaved, quiet, sober, and respectful in the presence of these things or values, even though they seem to you to be of little practical use. Transfer this situation to a metaphorical museum—a real-life circumstance perhaps connected with family or cultural values—and you will have decoded your dream.

See also **ANTIQUE**

Naked

Inhibitions belong to the emotions and the normal outer feelings. In contrast, the inner feelings are free from inhibition. Some people habitually see themselves as naked in their dreams, and this circumstance, as far as other dream characters are concerned, seems perfectly natural. Yet sometimes it seems to be an issue in itself. Where clothes symbolize the trappings of the psyche—the passions, the social disguises, the emotional veneer we tend to wear in company—nakedness symbolizes the absence of these features. So to dream that you are naked and unashamed in company means that in the dream you are presenting yourself as you really are, without pretense.

However, if your sensations in the dream are unpleasant and you feel the need to hide your nakedness, it implies that you have been forced by circumstances to drop your disguise; possibly an unfortunate situation that you have arrived at by acting against your own better judgment.

See also **CLOTHES**

Obstacles

Dream obstacles can take myriad forms and are limited only by your imagination. They draw attention to real-life obstacles that impede your progress. For clues, identify anything or anyone in the dream and apply this information to your life. You may not have recognized your real-life obstacle for what it is—for instance, your style of dress or social attitude may be impeding your career prospects.

See also **BAGGAGE**

Opponent

This is the dream archetype allied with the adversary and the assailant. The adversary is usually a characteristic of your self you would rather not face; the assailant is usually a challenging situation outside yourself. Decide where your opponent comes from. Your opponent may represent a real-life competitor, or may have arisen from your unconscious mind. Look for clues in your dream. The dream may point to a way to overcome a challenge in your life.

See also **ADVERSARY, ASSAILANT**

Painting

There are two basic types of painting. One is a practical way to cover things up, cloaking them in color. The other is the artistic depiction of an event, person, or scene—painting a picture. In the first case, as a rule, something is being made to look attractive; in the second, as a rule, something attractive is being made. In either case something is being presented in a new way, and this is the essence of the dream symbol. Much depends on who is doing the painting in the dream and what is being covered up or newly created: If you or someone you know are the painter, the meaning of the symbol should be clear enough.

See also **ART**

Paralysis

Sleep paralysis occurs sometimes when your dream becomes lucid and you know you are dreaming (see Chapter 5). You may feel as though you are paralyzed—trying to wake up or get out of bed but unable to move. This can be very alarming and could well be called a nightmare. If it happens frequently, there may be a medical reason. If not, try to connect it with any other features within your dream; the unpleasant sensation could be related to an equally unpleasant situation in real life that you are unable to shake. The dream should give you a clue about this. It may even offer you a solution to your problem.

See also **FEAR**

Parrot

Traditionally parrots are taught to speak without understanding what they are saying, and this will be the gist of your dream symbol. When trying to learn a foreign language, for instance, you may dream of a parrot perched on your shoulder. Perhaps the dream (by way of your inner feelings) is poking mild fun at you (it does happen!); but of course a young child learning to speak may repeat sounds that have not as yet been associated with their meaning. This is part of the learning process.

See also **BIRDS**

Mountains may represent a need to scale heights or overcome obstacles.

Path

One of the most ancient of dream symbols is your own path through life. Driving your car or riding your bike may have the same meaning. How the symbol is best interpreted depends upon what you encounter along the way and on the difficulty or ease of travel. These factors will reflect your own ability to cope with the problems you meet from day to day. Your path may be easy, indicating fortunate circumstances of fate; it may be uphill, downhill, or muddy; it may pass through overgrown patches, across fords, or through snow and ice. Symbols of this sort need decoding separately.

See also **DRIVING, FEET, JOURNEY, ROAD**

Pearl

A pearl of great price symbolizes a nonmaterial treasure. Pearls in nature are produced by oysters under the sea: in symbolic terms, deeply hidden within the emotions, at the very bottom of the personal mandala, within the concealing armor of an ancient, primitive lifeform, in the darkest part of the self—the personal shadow. When an oyster yields up its treasure, the dreamer will have found a means of penetrating the hidden emotions, re-creating the dark contents to make the self complete and whole. The spherical shape of a pearl, too, carries the significance of evolution and new creation.

See also **GOLD, TREASURE**

Pig

This is a symbol of highly variable significance, for pigs occupy a prominent place in the feelings of most people of the world. As a dream symbol, the impact will be powerful, but it will depend entirely on the dreamer's own cultural background. The pig is an intelligent creature with many similarities to humans. A wild boar occupies a different category and represents untamed animal passions, but a domestic pig will represent a familiar and valuable source of food to one person and, because of religious proscription, to another it will represent the epitome of evil, notoriously greedy, a living garbage can. Pink and naked, pigs and piglets as dream symbols can represent sexual peccadilloes. An interesting symbol, and one that calls for careful and tactful interpretation.

See also **ANIMALS**

Pit

One of the most basic of dream symbols. Remember that the dark lower half of the circle of the self, the yin, is the unconscious mind into which all the matters that have not been fully dealt with—thoughts, feelings, impressions—are pushed by the conscious mind. This is the symbolic pit, the storeroom of the subconscious, which the dreaming process is constantly working to clear out. The dream of the backyard pit recorded in Chapter 1 is a typical example: You probably have intended to throw your dirty and unwanted things into your dream pit, and the dream is telling you to deal consciously with the matters that affect you as they arise; don't push them away, hoping they will disappear. They won't! They continue to exist in the pit, where they can take on a new and frightening form; sooner or later they emerge and may disturb the waking mind. If you seem in danger of falling into a pit, you are being warned to tread carefully in some real-life situation. Take stock of your current situation and relationships and try not to depend too much on rules and regulations.

See also **ABYSS**

Playing

Whatever sort of game is being played in the dream, much of its significance depends on whether you, the dreamer, are taking part or merely watching. You may already have recognized the true significance of the dream game. If not, think in terms of the "rat race," the constant activity of work and play, and ask yourself: Are you playing the part you really want to in this game of life? There will probably be an important message for you hidden in this symbol. Are you overplaying or underplaying? Should you make more of an effort to join in group activities, or is it time to stand back and reappraise your lifestyle? Only you can decide.

See also **BALL, CARNIVAL, MARKET**

Police

Most people care about their own character, whether others see them as basically good or bad, preferring to give the positive impression of helping rather than hindering the rest of humankind, of following some unspoken rules of conduct through life. This is not the same as excessive morality: It is common humanity. For those who do care about their own character, and in particular if they have set out on a path of psychological individuation or spiritual attainment, the dream cop acts as a warning or safeguard against temptation. To dream of carrying a friendly policeman in your car means that you have made or are about to make a morally correct decision.

See also **UNIFORM**

Precipice

This stark symbol may be warning you of dangers ahead. If the track you have been following ends on the edge of a cliff, the message could scarcely be clearer. In more general terms, the precipice may be yet another symbol of the unconscious mind, the edge of awareness over which all unwanted and half-forgotten ideas are pushed out of sight. Whichever is the case in your dream, the symbol is warning you to take stock, whether in practical or in psychological terms, or both.

See also **ABYSS, PIT**

Procession

Are you taking part in the dream procession or merely watching? If you are watching, it may be reflecting your observation that everyone is taking a particular point of view—one you may not agree with and do not wish to endorse. If you are participating, the symbol may be implying that you are going along with the majority view, being swept along by the crowd, when it might be better for you to hold back and rethink your situation.

See also **CARNIVAL**

Quarrel

If you are quarreling with someone in your dream, although you may be convinced of your own position and feel very strongly about it, it usually turns out that you are the one in the wrong. Dreams are seldom required when you are in the right! In all probability, the dream is dropping the hint that you are being unreasonable or obstinate about something that is hurting your pride. Your inner feelings are never cloaked in pride; if you are the guilty one, they are well aware of it. If you have been arguing with someone in real life, an apology from you is probably called for.

See also **ABUSE, ACCUSATIONS**

Queen

If you are a woman, this dream symbol may have been borrowed from the collective unconscious by your own inner feelings. Are you the queen or are you merely watching or listening to her? And how is she behaving in the dream? She may represent yourself as you would like others to see you or she may represent a higher part of your own self and be able to offer you sound advice. Try to identify all the dream characters and incidents and relate them to real-life situations; this type of dream needs careful thought; it is sure to carry an important message connected to your relationships and attitude toward friends and colleagues.

See also **GODDESS, WISE PERSON**

Rail Trip

Nowadays a car trip signifies passage through life, the car representing an extension of the legs—the natural mode of transport. A journey by train, however, usually symbolizes a more definite movement from one place to another, a transition from one lifestyle to another. The meaning of this symbol does vary according to the dreamer's own experience of train journeys. People who normally commute daily by train may give this symbol an entirely different, less significant meaning.

See also **JOURNEY, PATH, ROAD**

Rainbow

According to the biblical account, God created a rainbow as a sign that there would be no more worldwide floods. It is said that a rainbow shines around the throne of God. Certainly it is the most beautiful natural phenomenon connected with the weather. Also, as it usually appears when rainstorms are at an end, and as it shines most brightly against dark clouds on the horizon, it has become naturally a symbol of relief from trouble. It signifies the end of an unpleasant or worrying period in your life and points to your hope for the future.

Rats

Some people keep rats as pets and love them—but most people see them as disease-carrying pests and are disgusted by the very idea of them. The truth is, of course, that they are just animals living their own lives. Their way of life brings them close to humans, and in order to thrive, they largely depend on human activities. Because of this attachment and because of the strong feelings they provoke, it is quite understandable that rats have come to symbolize these feelings in ourselves. Whatever you personally think of rats and whatever your feelings toward them are, when some act of your own makes you feel similar feelings, a dream rat may well emerge: It becomes a symbol for your own dubious behavior. In order to decode it, you need to search your memory, belief system, and experience.

See also **ANIMALS**

River

For centuries in the Christian tradition, the Jordan River has represented the barrier between life and death. Any river appearing as a dream symbol can have a similar meaning. More usually, however, a river signifies the flow of emotions; specifically, the flow of sexual desires. The image of a hermit living alone by a river is the symbol of someone suppressing sexual desires.

Crossing a river or looking at one with a view to crossing it, is a common dream experience for people who have consciously begun to travel along the path of psychological individuation or spiritual purification—that is, when the cycling process of their own personal self, expressed by the mandala, is in positive action and is working toward wholeness.

Of great significance is the nature or quality of your dream river: It may be a raging torrent, implying that the emotions and sexual feelings you experience are something to be feared by your conscious mind; or it may be a crystal-clear stream and wholly attractive; or perhaps it is muddy and rather unwholesome—a plain reflection of your waking views.

See also **FORD, WATER**

Road

This is one of the most basic of dream symbols—the course of your life, the way ahead. The surface of the highway itself will be significant—whether it is smooth and clear, rutted and full of holes, or littered with obstacles. This is how your current situation is being portrayed by your inner feelings. Everything you encounter along the dream road reflects your day-to-day experiences. The inner feelings may express themselves in parables; dreams are often the inwardly visible projections of these parables.

See also **JOURNEY, PATH, RAIL TRIP**

Rocks

A rocky place is typical of dream symbols expressing the life force of materiality when its implication is spiritual barrenness. A more down-to-earth interpretation is a period of hardship, which has to be followed through. To be traveling through a rocky place implies that this is a temporary phase that will soon be surmounted.

See also **MOUNTAIN, ROAD**

Rooster

Since prehistoric times the domestic rooster has earned its place as a symbol of awakening, of alertness, and thereby of coming to a new realization, a new dawning of awareness. Today, in dreams, the crowing cock still represents new understanding, but not necessarily something good to know about yourself. Sometimes it heralds doubt in place of mistaken confidence. Take the biblical account of St. Peter and the cock, which as predicted at its crowing made him realize his own failing—his disowning of Jesus. A new dawn brings new understanding, and this is at the root of the symbol: Wake up to the rooster's clarion call!

See also **BIRDS**

Ruins

Buildings are often a dream expression of an individual person—the potentially whole person. The building—that self—may have much-used living rooms, the scarcely used upstairs or higher, psychic or intellectual possibilities, and the basement of the unconscious mind, unvisited by the ego, where dark shadows may lurk. The symbol of a ruined house may suggest that a person we once depended on can no longer fill that need. An example dream in Chapter 5 used a ruined house to express a young man's overattachment to his mother. *The glory that once was* can also apply to religious buildings, portraying religious attitudes that are no longer valid for the dreamer.

See also **ABBEY**

Sand

This is a clear expression of barrenness. When life-giving water falls on sand, it usually drains away very quickly or makes a quagmire, and very few life-forms can live in it. If

Rivers often signify the flow of emotions and erotic yearnings.

you consider the world dream (Chapter 3), you will see that a sandy desert implies the absence of a sense of power. A feeling of helplessness experienced in your current situation is the most likely trigger for a dream in which you seem to be struggling through sand. Possibly a little more self-assertion or even aggression on your part is called for in real life. It is no use depending too much on the goodwill of others.

See also **DESERT**, **SWAMP**

Scrap Heap

The scrap heap is a collection of old items and trash, none of which is any longer of use. They may still be of interest; as memorabilia, they are fine. But this dream symbol could be telling you that you have been relying too much on past values, hanging on to ideas and relationships that are no longer relevant to your life. A reappraisal of your habits and lifestyle seems to be called for.

See also **BAGGAGE**, **OBSTACLES**, **PIT**

Sea

The collective unconscious has often been described as a vast sea of unknown depth, filled with psychic perceptions common to the whole of humankind. When you experience a great dream, especially when, very significantly, it arrives just before dawn, its images will most likely have been drawn from this psychic sea.

On a more everyday level, the sea represents ordinary human feelings: emotions, and sexual urges. You may be swimming in your dream sea and so, by implication, enjoying these things. You may be drowning in it, unable to cope with the immensity of it all. You may be tasting it tentatively or you may even be able to swallow the lot,

suggesting that in some way you have risen above your own urges.

See also **WATER**

Shack

A shed, hut, or some kind of small building—perhaps only large enough for one to enter at a time—is a potent and very strange symbol. When you enter this dream hut you are completely enclosed—closed in and shut off—by your own self, by your own passions and feelings and sensations, your own little world. It is often the symbol of illness or death, and you may experience this dream on behalf of someone close to you, as in the intuitive dreams in Chapter 7. When this person (or you) emerges, everything will be changed and the situation will call for major reorientation. This is the basic meaning of the symbol: The individual has become closed off and is probably undergoing some traumatic experience, finally to emerge with a new outlook, a new orientation, a new life—for better or worse.

See also **BARN**

Snake

A powerful symbol throughout human history and, no doubt, prehistory, too, the snake is, first, a symbol of temptation—originally, in the biblical sense, of rejecting the instinctive life of Eden in favor of human cleverness. Second, it is a symbol of eternal life, or more mundanely of perpetual youth or renewed vigor, as a snake sloughing its skin. Third, it is a symbol of "lowness," and thence of untrustworthiness. Fourth, it is a symbol of sex, by its perceived phallic shape. A dream snake might represent any of these things or simply a hidden danger to be wary of—a snake in the grass.

See also **ANIMALS**

Snow and Ice

Walking through snow and ice implies passing through a wintry, difficult time, but one that will, by its nature, shortly pass into spring. Steady progress through snow and frost and ice is usually a good omen of progress in the right direction. It advises patience on the part of the dreamer, and perseverance at whatever he or she is finding wearisome in waking life. As with most symbols, the meaning will be modified by the dreamer's personal experiences and expectations; but temporary hardship remains the common factor.

See also **FROST, GLACIER, JOURNEY, MOUNTAIN**

Statue

As a human likeness, which is also an object of materiality, the symbol of a statue may carry much the same meaning as a solitary standing stone—the personal self—and the urgent need for change within the psychic center of gravity. A statue may also represent an archetype that seems to have become petrified or frozen in time through disuse; a human function that has long been overlooked. The symbol may carry a phallic significance, particularly when it seems small enough to be held in the hand. Personal interpretation is required within the context of the dream.

See also **CARVINGS, IDOL**

Stitchcraft

Who is doing the stitching, such as embroidery, in your dream? Is it you, or somebody else? If you are the creative one, could it be that you have been less than completely honest with someone, making up "a fabric of lies" perhaps, or "embroidering a half-truth" to make something appear more presentable? It may not be a negative dream. The whole of nature might be represented by a complicated piece of embroidery—a universal tapestry—and your dream may be showing you how you fit into this intricate overall pattern. Whatever it was that triggered the dream, the image suggests that a complicated state of affairs exists. If the person doing the embroidery pierces his or her finger with the needle, the dream is letting you know that this person has made a misjudgment, and has no option but to face the (not too serious) consequences. Are you that person?

See also **ART**

Stone Circle

In many cultures this is an ancient mandala symbol of the self in its relation to the world and the solar system. It can also signify the family circle, particularly when the family is perceived as unyielding and morally stringent. There is frequently a sense of having to pass through the stones, as through a gateway, to a new understanding or level of being. The implication is one of ancient wisdom, waiting to be discovered. Whether the dream circle is large and well organized, such as Stonehenge, or merely a rough and overgrown circle of stones among the hills, will depend largely on the dreamer's own background and experience. The symbol is less complete when it features only one isolated standing stone. But it is still a powerful symbol of the self and usually accompanies the waking realization that a new religious outlook is required by the dreamer.

Store

A building containing various goods may stand as a symbol of materiality–all the good things available, but perhaps at the cost of personal integrity or spiritual attainment. The dream store can also represent the personal unconscious—the place normally hidden within your psyche where all your experiences and impressions are stored.

See also **BARN, EARTH, PIT**

Sun

Probably the most ancient and abiding symbol of life and spirituality, a rising sun signifies the rebirth of the psyche to a new understanding or opportunity. The sun shines on all aspects of life unless they are hidden from view, so sunshine can symbolize openness in behavior and relationships, depending on the context of the dream.

A setting sun marks the passing of an old era. It implies a sense of peace with longing and may symbolize the desire to seek higher principles of life. In the world mandala, the setting sun sinks into materiality before reemergence, and the symbol also calls for patience and acceptance on the part of the dreamer.

See also **ECLIPSE**

Swamp

A morass, a quagmire, a slough, a marsh, a bog, a muddy patch into which your feet are inclined to sink: This is a very clear symbol of a sticking point, perhaps a somewhat treacherous path you are taking through life, or a situation that is holding you back and impeding your progress—maybe even putting you in danger. The swamp or bog in a dream may be reflecting your own feelings about a real-life situation, or it could be carrying a warning of a sticky patch ahead, involving the need to take evasive action. A change of direction may be needed in your career.

See also **MUD**

Theater

A theatrical performance is not necessarily to be taken literally, and a theater is not the place in which to look for sincerity or truth. As a place of entertainment, it provides a sometimes welcome escapism, but it may also inspire fresh ideas and a new way of looking at old problems. Your dream theater carries all these implications; the characters in it are not to be taken at their face value.

See also **ACTING**

Thorns

Thorny bushes represent a hostile environment, the dangers and difficulties you expect to encounter on your way. They can also symbolize persecution and unfair discrimination if this is being experienced.

See also **CACTUS, OBSTACLES**

Toilet

There are often at least two ways of understanding dream symbols. For instance, suppose that you dream that you need a toilet quickly but you can only find ones that don't work, are too dirty to use, are too public, are incomplete, or are unusable for whatever reason.

This is quite a common dream. It may mean simply that you have an urgent physical need and your own ego is arguing with your inner feelings, the one saying, *I want to go now!* and the other replying, *You can't, because you are still asleep in bed!* The physical explanation is simple enough. But certainly, if you don't actually need to wake up and go to the toilet, there must be another explanation—the need for shedding impurities, both psychological and spiritual. Most people have faults they know they should get rid of but tend to find excuses for hanging on to. It is when this state of affairs becomes urgent that you will dream of a toilet that cannot be used.

See also **FORTRESS**

Treasure

Dream treasure is more likely to be valuable for its psychological or spiritual rather than its material benefits. If you have actually found the treasure in your dream, you should be able to identify the nature of this good fortune by its dream associations. On the other hand, if you merely think it is somewhere near and are searching for it, this treasure will probably already be within your own psyche: There are few treasures more precious than the discovery of your own inner self—your own soul.

See also **DRAGON, GOLD, JEWELS, PEARL**

Tsunami

This is a specialized aspect of water as a dream symbol. Waves of emotion or a great wave—a veritable tsunami—of sexual desire, are the implications to be read into it. You should recall what effect the wave had on the surroundings, on other people in the dream, on everything that was apparently nonself, and compare this with the effect that it had on you, the dreamer. If the wave swamps you and sweeps you away, it is time for serious reappraisal of your lifestyle. If you were not personally swamped by the wave, the implication is that, though the way ahead may be tricky, you will surmount your difficulties safely.

See also **WATER**

Tunnel

A dream journey underground represents traveling along your life's road while you have temporarily lost sight of the light. Then, for a while, you are completely in the dark. If you have been feeling baffled by a worrying situation in the family or at work, you may well experience this dream symbol. If you can see a glimmer of light in the distance, the prospect is good. If not, you have two options. You either fall back on your faith and submit to a situation you cannot alter or you take determined steps to find out exactly what this tunnel represents in real life, and battle to find a way out of it. However, the problem may be within your own psyche: An underground cavern, a hole, or any dark, unexplored place is usually a symbol of your personal unconscious mind. The dream may be predicting that your power of conscious thought is due to undergo some sort of trauma—probably a temporary glitch from which you should quickly recover.

See also **ABYSS, DARKNESS**

Unemployed

It is quite common to dream of seeming to have no active role to play in life. Sadly, in some cases this may reflect the true state of affairs, such as may happen when the dreamer has recently retired from work or been laid off. Or, there may simply be a fear of job loss in the dreamer's mind.

Quite understandably, the real loss of work leaves a void that needs to be filled. But sometimes, the dream occurs when the dreamer is in no danger of being out of work. In all cases, even when the dream reflects reality, the feeling of emptiness, uselessness, or lack of occupation may have another meaning. We may dream of others who are unemployed—long lines of people suffering the effects of a major economic crisis—a depression: Dreams often make use of word play, and this one may be referring to a real case of clinical depression.

In addition, there is a still deeper significance overriding these variations: Our waking hours may be fully occupied with all sorts of activities, but if our inner awareness is not active, there will still be a sense of emptiness or nonfulfillment. The dream may be urging you to look for a way to stir your inner awareness to life.

See also **LOST**

Uniform

Uniformity, or the wearing of a uniform for school, for work, or merely as a fashion statement is a way of classifying people into groups. A uniform implies equality within a certain set; adhering to whatever is expected of you. A dream uniform is likely to imply acting in a way that others would expect you to act or perhaps suffering the same fate that all the others of your particular set are inclined to suffer. Some people like the idea of being one of the herd; others much prefer to be individual. Whatever your own situation, these are the ideas to bear in mind when decoding your dream.

See also **CLOTHES**

Valley

This represents a solid situation that pens you in. It may well refer to a matter of physical health, when you are unable to do all the things you used to do. When the valley is shrouded with mist, or even thick fog, it is reflecting the fact that you cannot see any better way forward. Above all, a dream valley is a symbol of materiality itself—even your highest thoughts and deepest emotions cannot help you to escape its confines. If you cannot think of any immediate significance, take it as a signal that you need to seek a way forward that is less oppressive: The dream is telling you that your life is lacking spiritual influence. This is different from spiritualism, which will lead you ever deeper *into* the dream valley.

See also **FOG, JOURNEY, MIST, ROCKS**

Vase

A dream example in Chapter 2 featured a vase, which represented the hidden feelings of the person carrying or owning it. In this vase she could accept the offering of her friend—a bunch of flowers. In other words, she could allow him into her feelings, but she rejected his gift because she didn't want him to examine a hidden side of her nature too deeply. A vase is an ornamental container, something that is meant to be seen and admired, but whatever it contains may remain unknown and unseen. As a dream symbol, you could describe the vase in poetic terms as "the recesses of your heart."

See also **BARN, CUP, STORE**

Volcano

Assuming the dreamer has not been involved with a real-life volcano, it is a symbolic mountain that "blows its top"; a "ticking time bomb"; a "'powder keg waiting to explode"; fire and fury erupting out of what may have seemed a peaceful scene. All these symbols seem to be warning the dreamer to avoid disturbing someone who (or something which) may react violently if provoked.

See also **EARTHQUAKE**

A tidal wave or tsunami may refer to an actual occurrence or
may symbolize the dreamer's rising sexual desire.

Wall

A barrier that can be either a hindrance or a help, a wall can prevent your escape and block your way forward or it can keep intruders out. It can also guide your way as a marker, and even keep you safe, perhaps as the boundary on a mountain road in the dark. A dream wall as a barrier certainly makes a very clear point: You are being impeded in some way in your everyday life; your ambitions are being thwarted. Yet it may also give you a clue as to the best way forward—there may be a gate or a stile some little distance along, or the line of the wall itself may lead you to a better route toward your destination.

See also **DOOR**, **FENCE**, **GATEWAY**, **HEDGE**

Water

There are many forms that the water symbol can take—the sea, waves, rivers, streams, lakes, ponds, or wells, or drinking water in a cup or the hollow of the hand. Personal interpretation of the whole dream should never be neglected, even if the meaning of the symbol itself seems obvious. The feelings, the emotions, are symbolized in dreams by water; it follows that the clarity or murkiness of dream water is significant. Psychological clutter that has not yet been dealt with in the personal unconscious will darken and discolor the water with mud.

Clear water with coral, shells, and clean pebbles signifies crystal-clear emotions, with not too many psychological blocks. Murky water suggests you give attention to your inner condition; recording and analyzing your dreams is a good start. The first step toward solving a problem is often acknowledging that the problem exists.

In the symbolism of the East a hermit living on the banks of a mighty river is one who practices celibacy; in his case the river represents his sexual desires. In Western symbolism a river can represent death; crossing it means leaving life's passions behind. To experience difficulties in crossing a river or stream in your dream may mean that you are reluctant to abandon old sexual habits that you would be better off without. It may also mean that you are unwilling to experience your own feelings to the fullest and tend to switch off when emotional subjects are raised.

A restricted or contained area of water is likely to symbolize the inner self. A flower such as a water lily floating on the lake can point out that you are placing too much reliance on your intellect or practicing emotional self-control while neglecting the deep water of the personal unconscious beneath the flower. The personal shadow that lurks in the depths of the lake may be growing in strength. The subconscious mind can also be symbolized by a well, which carries a symbolic representation of a store of wisdom waiting to be drawn. To drink water implies that you are taking in whatever is being symbolized by the water; overcoming personal problems can be represented in this way.

The collective unconscious can be symbolized by a vast sea, and swimming in or tasting the water implies familiarity with its contents—perhaps even to the extent of drinking the entire sea! But a gentle drink of water held in the palm of the hand may symbolize a taste of wisdom, while appreciating the need to follow good advice.

See also **BOAT**, **BRIDGE**, **DROWNING**, **FORD**, **LAKE**, **RIVER**, **TIDAL WAVE**

Weeding

When any intelligent person has become aware of the need to get rid of various faults and features that have become deeply ingrained and is finding it far from easy, weeding a flower bed will often feature as a dream symbol. Long underground roots and mat-forming weeds invading other plants portray undesirable characteristics that may be affecting the dreamer's life very extensively, and they may be deeply rooted in the inner feelings. Patience and perseverance are called for.

See also **DIRT, EXCREMENT**

Wise Person

An archetype of the unconscious mind, the wise person is a part of the self that tends to be called upon when carefully thought-out decisions are needed. In dreams it may appear as a teacher, a doctor, the dreamer's own father, or some other authority figure, ready to give advice. It is associated with the images of the king, the goddess, and the hero.

See also **ADVICE, GODDESS, KING, QUEEN, HERO**

Witch

This is an archetype of the unconscious mind that corresponds to the personal shadow, and is a feature of the female self. The witch comprises all those hidden characteristics you are ashamed of, have denied, or would rather not consider your own. These have continued to exist on a subconscious level until they form a powerful presence—the female equivalent of Stevenson's evil Mr. Hyde—that can make itself known when its owner loses control. Of course, some people understand the term *witch* rather in the sense of "goddess," as legitimately expressing their sense of religion, the life of the planet, and their awareness of the possibility of inner development. Any apparent contradiction tends to reflect the usage of words rather than dream imagery.

See also **DEMON, GODDESS**

Wolf

A wolf features in a dream example in Chapter 5, where it represented a life situation in which the dreamer was harassed at work. Although rarely an actual risk to humans, for many centuries wolves have represented a threat—something we are afraid of and have no control over. There is a strong sexual connotation, too: We use the term to describe a womanizing man. The wolf can also represent an enemy ("a wolf in sheep's clothing") or starvation ("keeping the wolf from the door"). We may "throw somebody to the wolves" by making him or her a scapegoat. The term *wolf pack* can apply to any marauding band or predatory gang. The wolf is a much-maligned creature, as all wild dogs tend to be—but any of these varied meanings may be applicable to your dream wolf. Chances are, it will refer to some real-life situation that has been worrying you.

See also **ANIMALS**

Xenophobia

The fear of foreigners is not an unusual dream symbol, alas, and it involves becoming aware of suspicious or seemingly dangerous unknown and alien people approaching or surrounding the dreamer. Sometimes this only involves a vague feeling of being threatened by a foreigner who does not actually appear in the dream. There may be a suggestion of an actual phobia of this kind affecting the dreamer's waking personality, but more likely the dream will have been triggered by some disturbing event involving perceived aggression or an attack of some sort by people of a different nationality.

Within dreams, a witch may embody darker, hidden characteristics.

There is an example of this kind of dream in Chapter 1, which was triggered by international incidents during the 1970s. Since then, far more people have experienced xenophobic dreams in the wake of recent terrorist outrages. This dream symbol falls into the category of *dream opponent*: It includes an element of the adversary because the actual fear—the phobia the dream is drawing attention to—is a part of the dreamer's own psyche; it includes an element of the assailant, because that deeply held fear is based on an actual threat from real individuals. As in the example dream mentioned, your own dream may be pointing out the unreasonable nature of any un-thought-out reaction against perceived outsiders.

See also **ADVERSARY, ASSAILANT, OPPONENT**

Yoke

An ancient dream symbol, the yoke may still occur, usually in disguised form. Its implication is drudgery, enforced labor, slavery, and a general feeling of being hard done by. The original yoke controlled oxen pulling a plow or drawing a cart. As a modern symbol it may be transferred to a machine—a "donkey engine"—or to any draft animal, and it often appears in dreams triggered by marital problems: A bored wife may dream she is a workhorse, which she feels she has become. Sometimes a dream may involve a wedding gift in the form of a carved piece of wood or some other contrivance that in itself seems meaningless to the waking mind—and this of course is none other than the archetypal yoke itself.

See also **LADDER, LOST, OBSTACLES**

Zoo

As a dream symbol, the place where many different kinds of animals are kept usually represents the animal instincts of people in the collective sense. It may appear when the dreamer moves to a new area or begins a new life circumstance—a new job, a new school—where the people have seemed to be less well behaved, less moral, less inhibited, or more sexually expressive than expected.

Of course, this stems from the dreamer's own perceptions of others. But the symbol can also imply a place where all the dreamer's animal passions are confined—a compartment of consciousness within the psyche of any individual, but probably of the dreamer personally. When someone is setting out on a truly spiritual path, the zoo symbol may appear as an expression of this compartment (most people normally live on a materialistic level, and animals—or even plants—can represent a step up on the spiritual ladder; see the discussion of the world dream in Chapter 3). Beneath it all, of course, people *are* animals—in the sense that they are largely governed by animal energy and automatic reactions. So in this sense, the zoo can be seen as a symbol of powerful constructive passions—a stepping-off point from which ambitions can be achieved.

See also **ANIMALS, FARM**

Nine

DREAM EMOTIONS

A change came o'er the spirit of my dream.

Lord Byron, "THE DREAM"

Remembering the spirit or the overriding emotion of your dream can help greatly in your interpretation. When you awaken from a particularly vivid dream, the feeling usually stays with you for some time and you may also remember that these feelings underwent a change at some point during the course of your dream. Make a careful note of this. It will contain vital information to help you to decode the message. The following are some of the most common theme moods to help jog your waking memory.

Abandonment, Forsakenness, Rejection

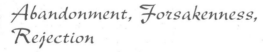 Of course, your dream may relate clearly to some real-life situation; and if it seems to contain no answer or solution, it may simply be expressing your own feelings, disappointment at being let down. If you feel abandoned or rejected in the dream and there is no real-life equivalent that you can see, try

to recapture the mood of the dream. Who or what has abandoned you? What was your dream situation as a result?

The emotion is closely allied to the dream symbol of being lost and may be pointing out that you seem to have lost your way in life. Again, if there is no obvious meaning involving your career or family or relationships, the dream may refer to a spiritual abandonment: In effect, you have abandoned or rejected yourself—your own nonmaterial higher self that can guide you through life if you let it. A dream of this nature gives a clear hint that you need to seek and follow a more spiritual path, and your dreams will point the way if you study and record them carefully.

Perhaps somebody else in your dream is expressing these powerful emotions. Perhaps you feel you have abandoned someone else. If the dream characters are real people and known to you, the meaning of the dream will be fairly obvious. The nature of abandonment may be practical rather than emotional. The feeling may have been projected by the person feeling abandoned, and you have picked them up in your dream. All the dream details need very careful consideration. If someone is feeling betrayed and in need of your friendship, don't let this person down!

It sometimes happens that a powerful feeling of abandonment or betrayal reflects your own feelings of guilt about something that may have happened long ago, over which you had no real control. If you can make amends, it might be as well to do so. If not, and if a feeling of guilt persists, try to feel deeply within yourself that you are not to blame for whatever occurred. If your feelings are sincere, it may well be that you will receive a further dream that will balance your feelings and relieve the sense of guilt.

Acceptance, Submission, Patience

If you experienced a powerful emotion of resignation or acceptance during your dream (or in a significant part of it), the implication is that you can trust the dream and put your faith in it. It may be indicating a positive message, which has already been accepted by your inner feelings—the source of dream imagery—but not yet by your everyday, outer feelings. Bearing this mood in mind, try to analyze the dream in the usual way. Trust whatever conclusion you reach; probably it is teaching you something very valuable. Try to look at the dream source as something higher than your own conscious awareness and accept it as an unknown place filled with wisdom.

Affection

Dreams about real people whom you feel affection for may reflect this affection.

However, sometimes you may awaken with feelings of affection after a dream about explicitly unpleasant things, people, or situations. This can seem very puzzling—but if you look at it as a case of misplaced affection, the message of your dream may become clearer. Your own inner self may be pointing out some characteristic or fault, perhaps, that your waking thoughts are unwilling to accept.

Are you being true to yourself? Try to look at your attitude from other people's point of view. Affection should be the presiding emotion among family and friends. You may be hanging on to a characteristic that your family and friends find unpleasant.

Aggression, Confrontation

In a dream the feeling of aggression tends to suggest a psychic imbalance or an unresolved conflict on the part of the dreamer. Sometimes the first part of a complicated dream will have aggression as its theme. Then the second part may well involve a change of spirit, and the predominant feeling of reconciliation or contentment may take over.

In such cases the dream may be pointing out a solution to a stressful situation in real life. If the feeling of aggression persists, however, even when wide awake, it may be pointing to deeply hidden feelings of guilt. The subject matter of the dream needs analyzing very carefully to decode the message.

Aggression in real life is a way of discouraging unwelcome advances from unwanted people. In the language of dreams, aggression may indicate a characteristic the dreamer does not want to face up to in waking life.

Amusement

Merriment often features in children's dreams. In most adult dreams, however, a genuine feeling of amusement is rather unusual, especially if the dream stems from the inner feelings. This is not because this higher emotional center lacks a sense of humor. Rather, it is because the function of our dreams is to instruct rather than entertain. An overall mood of amusement may occur during a balancing dream, pointing out that you have been taking some situation or incident too seriously. Real amusement is most likely to occur in a wish-fulfillment or lucid dream, in which you are aware you are dreaming and begin to manipulate the dream events. If this is the case, the dream itself is unlikely to be of value to the developing self.

Anger, Fury, Rage

Anger can sometimes actually be seen in a dream, or in a waking vision, appearing like a dark cloud issuing from an angry character's mouth. It may sometimes be detected as a rotten-plant smell.

Dream anger is often expressed when someone, perhaps quite unconsciously, points out a personal characteristic that may be acting as a barrier to smooth psychic functioning; he or she may have hinted at a flaw in the character of the person displaying the anger. Sometimes the emotion is transferred, so that the person who triggered it appears to be the angry one.

Dream anger of this type means that the psyche acknowledges the fact that change is needed but is unwilling to face up to it in waking life. Angry dreams always need personal interpretation by thinking about each element and theme to identify the mental or emotional barriers that exist. Righteous indignation in a dream may develop into uncontrollable fury. When this occurs in the dream world it can be taken as a lesson to be learned—something is wrong and needs to be put right.

Extreme anger is a destructive emotion. When you experience fury in your dream, you may wake up with pounding heart and confused thoughts, feeling almost as if you are ready to commit murder! But although the dream incident may have been outrageous enough to seem to merit so violent a reaction, you will probably already have realized that in practice, in waking life, it would achieve nothing of value to act out this rage. Indeed, it may well make a bad situation worse. The dream emotion may be warning you to adopt a more reasonable approach to life's problems.

Anxiety, Concern

This is one of the major mood themes accompanying what are probably the most commonly experienced types of dream. Anxiety or concern dreams express exactly a concern over some state of affairs—a period of doubt, anxiety over a future the dreamer cannot foresee. A concern-type dream in itself offers no solution. Yet on numerous occasions, the course of a dream will change—and anxiety gives way to relief, hope, or joy, when some plain solution to the problem emerges.

Apprehension, Foreboding

This dream emotion is closely related to anxiety, but tends to be subtler, more abstract. Feelings of approaching doom during a dream relate to vague fears at the back of the mind. During the course of such a dream, these feelings are liable to change to feelings of relief or reassurance, indicating that a solution to whatever is troubling the dreamer is being portrayed. Feelings of this nature are typical of dreams in which the dreamer seems to be lost (see LOST in the previous chapter), and may also relate to questions of faith.

Arrogance, Superiority

This is a rather unpleasant emotion, whether experienced awake or while dreaming. Such a dream may reflect a mistaken attitude you have adopted in waking life. Arrogant feelings of superiority in a dream may not be portraying your normal everyday attitude. The dream emotion may be pointing out that you need to cultivate more self-confidence, or suffer from unnecessary feelings of inferiority in your dealings with others. Such feelings often feature in plant-nature dreams (refer back to Chapters 3 and 4) oriented toward power seeking, which amounts to much the same thing as suffering from habitual feelings of inferiority. The dream needs analyzing very thoughtfully.

Conscience, Feelings of Guilt

The inner self is the seat of conscience, and your inner feelings or, as some would say, "the higher emotional center" of the psyche represents the source of dream images, the place where dream incidents and symbols are normally selected for projection within your own awareness. Small wonder, then, that dreams frequently express matters of conscience—even in the case of individuals who do not normally seem to have any conscience whatsoever (perhaps especially so in their case).

Matters worthy of censure, blame, or guilt sometimes tend to be pushed away by the conscious mind. When this happens, of course they do not disappear. They are filtered down into the hidden receptacle of the personal unconscious, where they are sifted and sorted by the inner feelings. They are then later released or presented to the conscious mind in the form of dreams.

It is inevitable that conscience dreams are mainly experienced by those who do not seem particularly conscientious in waking life: Many conscience dreams are concerned wholly with the feelings of others. It is so easy to hurt someone's feelings without even realizing it, only to have the matter brought to your notice in a dream. In this type of dream you may seem to be physically assaulting the one whose feelings have been hurt. Valuable lessons about getting on with others can be learned in this way.

Contempt, Disgust

No matter the identity of the people you have been dreaming about or the subject matter of the dream, if your strongest memory of that dream is your own feeling of contempt, you need to look into this dream and its interpretation very carefully and honestly. To feel contempt for someone else is to feel "holier than thou," and this is always a dangerous attitude to hold. The dream may well be offering you a piece of friendly advice: to be broad-minded in the future, to try to see things more from the other person's point of view.

Despair, Mourning

There are two possible ways to cope with sorrow and bereavement. You can maintain an unflinching public manner and attitude, bottling up your feelings, shunning any display of emotions, or you can collapse in floods of tears, mourn, wail and howl, beat your breast and tear your hair. These are both clichés, of course. But it has been said that people who display their grief most readily are able to return to living a normal life that much more quickly. A dream in which you experience despair may act as a form of catharsis, allowing you to release pent-up emotions that are a problem for you.

Doubt, Distrust, Indecision

These emotions can fill your dream and remain with you after you awaken. If the dream itself featured a personal real-life situation, plainly it needs considering very carefully: There may be good reason to tread cautiously. Vague feelings of misgiving and doubt without any apparent cause can indicate that you have reached a crossroads in your life and need to consider the way you intend to go. Take care not to be forced into making a rash decision, and try to avoid being too trusting or gullible. It often happens, however, that feelings of doubt early on in a dream can give way to feelings of certainty and relief in the latter part. This can prove greatly reassuring in your real life.

Exasperation, Irritation

This sort of feeling often accompanies dreams of family and colleagues and is typical of relationship dreams. It may be that you have been expecting too much of them, and the dream is urging you to be more easygoing in relationships. Everybody falls short of perfection, and nobody wants to be thought of as a control freak trying to control other people's lives.

Hate

Hatred is a totally negative and destructive emotion, one that has no place at all in well-adjusted people. If the hatred you experience in the dream is projected by another person and directed toward you, it is probably because your own conscience is troubled over some action, omission, or attitude that calls for urgent attention.

On the other hand, if you are the one feeling and projecting the hatred toward others in the dream, again it is likely that you are the culprit, and it is your own conscience calling out for investigation by your everyday thoughts and feelings. Your real-life relationships may have reached a confrontational phase, disrupted, perhaps, by something in your character that you do not want to face openly.

At all events, this dream emotion is a warning for your own benefit: Try to turn feelings of hatred and loathing to love and understanding. If you can do this, most of your problems will disappear. The next time you are ready for sleep, ask yourself for another dream that will help you turn the hatred into empathy and love, and that will clear the air. From personal experience I know this can happen; when it does, it will represent a turning point in your life.

Helplessness

Not only in dreams, but in real life, too, all of us have experienced the feeling of helplessness: helpless to alter events, to improve an unsatisfactory situation, to assuage another's brash actions, to avoid an unpleasant fate. When this sort of feeling becomes too powerful, and helplessness is affecting your life, your dreams will certainly reflect this fact and warn you about it. Write down the details of your dream and analyze it carefully. There may well be a solution hidden within its symbolism. So look for the clues that need your concentrated attention to decode.

Horror, Terror

Horror stories and movies usually involve imaginative horrors that arise from outside the people concerned, but they are not really frightening because they are not real. Dream horrors, it could be said, are also unreal, but they are far more disturbing than fictional fears because they almost always arise from inside the dreamer. Most likely, horrors that feature in a dream involve aspects or characteristics that were already there. They are hidden within your unconscious mind and are matters you do not want to face up to in real life.

If you think them through, some of the dream symbols described in this book—such as the abyss, the antagonist, and the assailant—will almost certainly yield powerful clues when decoding the cryptic message that is the substance of your horror dream. Your unconscious mind contains all the images you dread the most.

Reassurance, Relief

Dreams are frequently divided into two or more parts or episodes. It often happens that the concern, puzzlement, or worry you feel in the first part of the dream gives way to a feeling of reassurance as the scene changes and the dream story unfolds. This implies that a solution to the problem, whatever its nature, is already being formulated by your inner feelings and the worry of it is being eased. Even though your waking brain may not immediately grasp the full significance or meaning of the dream, chances are, the message was received and understood by the unconscious part of your mind, which filters thoughts during the day and works to set your conscious mind at rest. The reassuring dream emotion may herald an improvement in your day-to-day fortunes.

Ten

INTERPRETING YOUR DREAMS—A SUMMARY

Now, said the interpreter... bear well in mind what thou hast seen.

John Bunyan, THE PILGRIM'S PROGRESS

Never forget that dreams usually have more than one layer or set of meanings. As Freud pointed out, they have a *manifest content*—the obvious sequence of events and images that the dreamer sees and remembers, and the emotions that may accompany them; and they have a *latent content*—the hidden meaning of these things. The more deeply buried the latent meaning, the more significant it is likely to be for the dreamer's own understanding and well-being.

As mentioned earlier, a dream is rather like a political cartoon: Someone other than the dreamer will be politically ignorant; he or she will have no idea of the events leading up to the dream, and the significance of those events to the dreamer. The cartoon, or in this case the dream itself, will be no more than an amusing picture. Only you, the dreamer, can know about all the personal details (the political significance of the cartoon) in the form of your past experiences, your relationships, your thoughts and feelings.

It follows that, while someone else can analyze the dream, only you are in a position to interpret your own dream satisfactorily. A book such as this, or a person who specializes in dreams, can point out the usual significances to be attached to dream symbols—the images that make up the manifest substance of the dream—and this knowledge will help to understand the general picture. But only you, the dreamer, can know the emotions, thoughts, and the past experiences underlying these manifest contents; only you can trace the association of ideas that might stem from them.

Association of Ideas

The psychological game of free association can be useful when analyzing and interpreting your own dreams. Traditionally, psychiatrists use a list of words specially selected to lead toward likely human-problem areas; reluctance to give the first answer that comes to mind is taken as a significant pointer to some kind of mental block. But when interpreting your own dream, you must act on your own, and there is really no need for that thoughtful pause.

On your own, nothing but your own pride can stand in the way. If you involve a friend or relative in tracing your associations of ideas or train of thought, you may quite understandably pause occasionally before answering—you will be on the defensive because of a natural reluctance to embarrass or be embarrassed, to show yourself in a bad light, to "give the game away." Dreams—or the inner feelings, the higher emotional center that selects most of our dream images—often make use of puns, double meanings, word play, and innuendo. It is exactly this kind of cryptic dream language that can yield secrets through the word association game.

Associations of ideas have few basic variations. They may relate to general similarities that spring to mind: cloud—sky; leaf—flower. Or to preconditioned association, or continuity: book—read; bottle—beer. Or to natural opposites: black—white; big—little. But in this case you will use all the items that you recall as featuring in the dream and, one at a time, follow each idea individually, pursuing it indefinitely along the same track. Your word associations will be wholly personal, and all those ideas will relate to your own experiences; even so, you may be led into areas where you feel uneasy, especially when half-forgotten memories are being uncovered. You may come to a place where you want to pause without necessarily running out of possible words to use; you might find yourself selecting a more pleasant alternative—and this pause could be hiding the problem or characteristic that has already been identified by the inner feelings. This pregnant pause could be pointing out the hidden meaning of your dream—something that you wanted to keep hidden from everyone—including yourself!

Remembering and Recording

In the first place, you will need to record your dream accurately while it is still fresh in your memory—preferably as soon as you wake up. Keep an open notebook with pencil or ballpoint close by your bed. You might want to scribble something in the dark, or even with your eyes shut! Try not to embellish any details in an attempt to make the dream more interesting or flattering. After all, pleasant though it may be, the immediate aim is not to be flattering but to uncover and decode the dream message. It may be very important to you.

In my view, the ultimate aim is to understand your own self and become a better person for it. Make careful notes of your feelings during each phase of the dream: whether you felt at ease or under stress or experienced feelings such as guilt, doubt, puzzlement, anger, or amusement. Refer to the entries on these dream emotions in the previous chapter—they are important pointers.

The practical nature of a dream object is only one aspect of it. If a wall has barred your way in the dream, the important thing may be not so much the nature or composition of the wall as the accompanying emotions you felt while trying to climb or bypass it and your feelings toward what might lie beyond. The wall itself is the manifest symbol, but your feelings may indicate something of its latent content, the real nature of the barrier impeding your progress, which may equate with any difficulties you are currently encountering in real life.

Nonself dreams, in which you seem to have become another person, and dreams that relate to the collective unconscious are sure to include details that do not seem to relate to you personally. However, most of the dreams you experience will be straightforward, personal dreams, relating to your own life and relationships. They are sure to include matters that have significance for you alone; only you can explore this type of dream thoroughly.

In writing down your dream story as it happened, you will probably find it includes a theme and series of incidents. Try to isolate each dream incident and identify the symbols involved. If recognizable emotions or powerful feelings were involved, look these up in Chapter 9 and try to relate them to the incidents. For the next step, look up the appropriate dream symbols and their possible interpretations. Some dreams can be understood quite readily in this way.

For instance, Sarah dreamed that she was forever searching through her wardrobe to find something suitable to wear, but nothing seemed right. She felt a desperate need to get dressed up, go out, and take an active part in all the action out there, but she seemed hopelessly stuck. This dream recurred several times.

If your dream is similar to this, you will no doubt look up the symbol *clothes* and learn that in dreams your clothes usually represent your personality. You will also look up the discussion of recurrent dreams in Chapter 2 and note that these usually indicate a personal psychological problem that needs facing. Sarah's dream was pointing out that she lacked self-confidence because she was afraid of not fitting in, was fearful of what people might think of her if she presented the wrong image. Once she realized this, Sarah came to a decision, determined that people must accept her at face value, warts and all. She regained her lost confidence, became more assertive, and never looked back.

Complicated Dreams

For more complicated dreams, it will seldom be enough to rely on symbols alone for interpretation. Take the case of Paul, an architect in his mid-sixties who had been having trouble with his heart and was worried lest he would not be able to complete his latest project—one he was very proud of and held high hopes for. This was his dream:

I was driving along in my car. The road was very potholed and muddy. I came to a crossroads and stopped, not sure which way to go. A railroad ran close to the road, and an empty train was standing there. The old engine was wheezing and sounded as if it were breaking down. The engineer got out of his cab and stood there uncertainly. He was an elderly man and wore a uniform of faded red. Then another man appeared at the side of the road, a stranger, well dressed and authoritative. He introduced himself, but I immediately forgot his name. I asked him the best way to go. He got in the car with me and pointed out the best road, and I drove on. Then we came to a town and I stopped. My passenger advised me to buy some flowers, and I bought a bunch of lilies. I asked him his name again, but again I forgot it, and I murmured to myself, "This man is filling my mind with forgetfulness." As we stood there, a funeral procession came by. Then, suddenly, the people taking part in the procession stopped, abandoned whatever they were carrying, and strolled away, chatting casually among themselves. I realized that this had been merely some sort of dress rehearsal and not a real funeral.

The dream symbols involved included a car (representing Paul's own journey through life); the road (the course of that journey—at present going through a rough patch); a train (a potential final journey—or a potential public journey of discovery, perhaps, for the many people who might eventually use the building Paul was working on); a wise person (the well-dressed man—an archetype belonging to Paul's own psyche and a source of personal knowledge and guidance); a funeral (the essence of his worry—was it real or not?). Additionally, both the engine and the engineer seemed old and decrepit (would they be able to make it to the station?), and the engine driver was dressed in red, a color suggesting blood and possible illness. Emotions were present, too, changing three or four times during the course of the dream. Paul noted that there were two main themes, two distinct parts of the dream, first involving concern and, later, reassurance.

For a complicated dream such as this, it is helpful to set it out in diagrammatic or tabular form, step by step. Doing this helped Paul realize that his fears were unnecessary:

Overall Theme	Dream Sequences	Waking Conclusions	Changing Emotions
Concern	Driving a car	Paul's own journey through life	Anxiety
	Bumpy road	Going through a worrying period	
	Crossroads	Uncertainty, indecision	
	Empty train	Potential for public interaction with his unfinished project	
	Wheezy old engine	Doubts about the future	
	Elderly engineer	Lack of physical confidence	Doubt
	Red uniform	Threat of ill health	
Reassurance	Wise man	Paul respects the wisdom of his fellow traveler	
	Indicates correct route	His own higher self can direct progress	
	Forgets name	A source of wisdom not available to the conscious mind	Puzzlement
	Advice to buy flowers	By buying lilies Paul accepts the inevitability of death	Acceptance
	"Filling my mind with forgetfulness"	Exchanges anxiety for deference	
	Funeral procession	Paul's fears being faced	
	Funeral disbanded	His fears are unfounded	Relief

Many dreams of an informative nature are divided into two or more distinctive parts or themes. In this case, the first part reflects Paul's worries about his overall life situation as he was experiencing it at the time. He was not a hypochondriac, but perhaps he had been worrying too much over his health. Certainly he was very proud of his creative work and wanted others to appreciate it to the full. The second part of the dream expressed reassurance—offering an answer to the major question that had been troubling him. The turning point was expressed by the crossroads—not knowing which route to take, and the route in this case was a matter not of actual direction, but of mental attitude. Paul could make himself really ill by worrying about the future or he could adopt a more submissive attitude to life, a calm acceptance of the principle *What will be, will be.*

His own higher intuitive self came to the rescue at the turning point in the dream, in the form of the archetype of the wise person who knew better than the everyday mind how to deal with life's little worries. As he was part of Paul's own psyche, of course, he was sharing his journey. Paul accepted him as a passenger without question, trusted him and thought he deserved respect, following his advice on which route to take. When they reached town, the stranger acted rather like a doctor diagnosing Paul's state of health, and Paul accepted the diagnosis. The doctor is another common role played out in dreams by the advisor archetype. Paul's inability to remember the stranger's name, though he was told it twice, stresses that this mysterious figure belongs to Paul's own unconscious mind and could not really be made conscious; his identity would have to remain a mystery.

If there is a long-term lesson to be learned from Paul's dream, it must be: It is no use worrying over things you cannot control. The outcome of any truly meaningful dream shows that intuitive knowledge is to be acquired not by striving, but by submitting to some sort of higher power—whether that power resides in your own unconscious mind or elsewhere in the universe.

Now, with what you will have learned, dream with knowledge and awareness, and discover this power for yourself.

INDEX

About the Author

Ray Douglas has been recording and interpreting dreams for more years than he cares to remember. He has experienced for himself every type of dream described in this book and was the first person to formulate the progressive development of dreams throughout the sleeping period. In addition, it was he who made the amazing discovery that our dreams sometimes reflect the underlying dreaming world of nature, the secret life of Gaia—our world seen as a vast, living, self-regulating organism, an entity of rock, water, soil, plants, animals, and humans. Most people within their own subtle natures are on the way down from the original quality of humanity, the truly human condition of a newborn child. Eventually, in spiritual terms, they reach the rock bottom of materiality, and their dreams may indicate this somewhat startling fact.

Whatever our race or individual status, according to Ray Douglas, the innermost self takes in the subtle contents of nature, experiencing successive layers of soul quality. In adulthood, having touched bottom, the inner self should set out again on the second stage of its journey—a return to the source. In mirroring these various levels, our dreams are intended to provide a source of wisdom, a guide through life. It is useful to take dreams seriously; unfortunately most are either ignored or forgotten. Indeed, far from taking them seriously, some people have even learned to manipulate them as a form of amusement.

Just as there are many vehicles we can ride, there are many different ways of understanding divine truths. Recording and understanding our dreams is one of them. For the past forty years Ray Douglas has been following the spiritual path of Subud—*Susila Budhi Dharma*—which has helped many people in the pursuit of their spiritual goal and given them tools to become acquainted with the inner feelings—the chief source of dream imagery.